Praise for *Transform: How Leading Companies Are Winning with Disruptive Social Media*

Social technology is core to T-Mobile's vision and road map. In *Transform*, Chris offers both a complete mastery of social technology and step-by-step instructions for how companies can win in this space.

> —Scott Tweedy, Vice President Customer Service and Sales, T-Mobile

Every business in the world is affected by the changing nature of work, rapid pace of innovation, and disruption occurring all around us. Organizations realize that to stay ahead, they have to approach their technology, culture, and processes differently. The tools and frameworks that Chris Morace describes in *Transform* are vital for companies looking to win in today's competitive market.

> —Aaron Levie, Cofounder and CEO, Box

When I need to better understand something about how software, particularly social software, is being used by companies, Chris Morace is the first person I go to. In *Transform*, he's distilled what he knows and made it accessible it to a wide audience. My advice is simple: read it if you want to empower your people and improve your organization.

> —Andrew McAfee, Principal Research Scientist, MIT's
> Center for Digital Business, and author of *Enterprise 2.0*
> and coauthor of *Race Against the Machine*

There's a revolution happening in corporate America. To succeed in this revolution, knowledge has to be shared. You need a social platform, one like Chris Morace describes, that knows what you want to know, presents ideas to you, and enables you to connect to the right people. In very large companies like ours, a social business platform allows us to recognize what we know and gets us to the heart of what we are trying to make happen.

> —Debby Hopkins, Chief Innovation Officer, Citi

As the social business revolution enters the next wave, organizations that missed the first wave will want to know the secrets of success of the market leaders and fast followers. Chris Morace's book provides the lessons learned by some of the most successful early adopters. This is a must-read book for any organization seeking to improve how work gets done, the customer experience, and the innovation cycle.

> —R. "Ray" Wang, Principal Analyst and CEO, Constellation Research, Inc.

Disruptive technologies are transformative by their nature. They alter how we work and how we live. In this extremely well-written book, Chris Morace captures the process and effort that it takes to provide disruptive technologies flawlessly. Stop reading this endorsement and go buy the book, or the next disruption may be your own!

—Paul Greenberg, author of the bestselling *CRM at the Speed of Light: Social CRM Strategies, Tools, and Techniques for Engaging Your Customers* and President, The 56 Group, LLC

More than a decade ago, *The Cluetrain Manifesto* described a powerful new global conversation between customers and companies, foreshadowing a massive power shift. Now, the social/mobile/cloud technologies that enable these new relationships at scale are accessible to all. In *Transform*, Chris Morace provides an indispensable guide that describes how to win in the new customer-empowered marketplace.

—Mark Yolton, Vice President Digital Strategy Enablement, Cisco

The world has changed; how we create value has changed. But, have you? If the industrial era was about building things, the social era is about connecting things, people, and ideas. In *Transform*, you learn how to be a talent-enabled, purpose-filled, and community-driven organization. Then, and only then, will you thrive.

—Nilofer Merchant, TED speaker, business innovator, and author of *The New How* and *11 Rules for Creating Value in the #Social Era*

Knowledge and information are the raw materials of innovation and competitive advantage in the global economy. Chris Morace makes a strategic case for social business then combines it with the experiences of real companies that have used social to unlock the value of their knowledge and turn it into innovative products and services.

—Jon Bidwell, Chief Innovation Officer, Chubb & Son, Inc.

Transform

Transform

How Leading Companies Are Winning with Disruptive Social Media

CHRISTOPHER MORACE
WITH SARA GAVISER LESLIE

New York   Chicago   San Francisco   Athens   London
Madrid   Mexico City   Milan   New Delhi
Singapore   Sydney   Toronto

1 2 3 4 5 6 7 8 9 0   DOC/DOC   1 0 9 8 7 6 5 4 3

ISBN   978-0-07-182659-4
MHID   0-07-182659-9

e-ISBN   978-0-07-182392-0
e-MHID   0-07-182392-1

This publication is designed to provide accurate and authoritative information in regard to the subject matter covered. It is sold with the understanding that neither the author nor the publisher is engaged in rendering legal, accounting, securities trading, or other professional services. If legal advice or other expert assistance is required, the services of a competent professional person should be sought.

—*From a Declaration of Principles Jointly Adopted by a Committee of the American Bar Association and a Committee of Publishers and Associations*

McGraw-Hill Education books are available at special quantity discounts to use as premiums and sales promotions or for use in corporate training programs. To contact a representative, please visit the Contact Us pages at www.mhprofessional.com.

To John Rizzo, who understands the power of belief
and transformation.

CONTENTS

FOREWORD

Everyone who works in a corporation deals with the same issue: how to drive revenue and increase the bottom line. That means higher productivity, better business processes, faster decision making, fewer meetings, less travel, less e-mail, and less time wasted.

CEOs and CIOs have tried to deliver business value by spending massive amounts of money and time selecting exactly the right technology for their organization. This worked for a while. The entire industry got really good at automating thousands and thousands of business processes with layers of management, protocols, and silos—pulling every bit of cost imaginable out of the business. But though we've spent billions of dollars and become great at automating the enterprise, we've overlooked something critically important.

Consider the fact that businesses today are spending 70% of their annual operating budget on their people. Yet, what have we done for them? The vast majority of employees still work with old tools and slow bureaucratic, time-sucking processes, which require countless meetings. In McKinsey's groundbreaking social economy study of July 2012, it was found that people waste 28 hours per week doing mindless tasks like responding to e-mails, searching for information, and sitting in on irrelevant meetings.

Why wouldn't we want to make an investment in our most important asset—our people? And how can we bridge the gap between the way people now communicate and engage in their personal lives and the way they work every day?

The new workforce is social. They grew up on Facebook, LinkedIn, Skype, and Twitter. They're used to getting instant responses from their networks via IM and group texts. E-mail, however, is an ancient tool. Younger workers don't know how to set up—let alone check—voice mail when the light flashes on the desk phone. They are mobile; smartphone adoption in the United States is faster than any other major technology shift, including television, the Internet, e-mail, and even radio. They live in the cloud; they need information whenever and wherever they are across all their devices. Who has the time or inclination to be chained to a workstation? They don't want to use an e-mail system that's 40 years old, an ERP system that's 25 years old, and a CRM application that's 15 years old.

It is time to turn the Titanic. The enterprise is replatforming due to the convergence of cloud, mobile, big data, and social, and it's changing the way work gets done—forever. Social enterprise platforms that combine these technologies are drastically transforming business cultures and creating business value. Instead of just servers and network systems connecting, in the new world of work, people, places, and content are now connecting to work better. When employees can navigate this information, get personalized results, and consult the social graph to find more relevant information, they can spend more time doing what they love—and get paid to do it! Instead of wasting time, they can code more, develop more, sell more, market more, and innovate faster.

As this book makes clear, the business value of social is real. I've always believed that the social era will be the most important transformation that happens in the enterprise. But until now, we've heard too much talk about social for social's sake. Today, we've turned the page on social software in the enterprise. It's not just about fun; it's not just about technology; and it's not Facebook for the enterprise. You need to know why you are using social technologies and platforms to grow revenue, increase profitability, and spur innovation. If done right, social will become the mission critical technology in any business.

Forward-thinking enterprises recognize that to advance and engage this new workforce, you can't use old tools to do new things. This book is for every company that wants to learn how to retool around social, mobile, and cloud, unlock the silos, and break down the barriers with big data. Hundreds of companies are already using social business tools to create value. These companies were once in the exact place where you are today. This book shows you how to follow their lead.

We are still at the beginning of the social enterprise evolution. But the rising tides of the new workforce cannot be ignored. We deserve business systems that unlock creativity and human potential. We are right on the cusp of changing the way work gets done.

Tony Zingale
CEO, Jive Software

ACKNOWLEDGMENTS

Christopher Morace:
I've learned many things while writing this book, but the most important is that publishing requires relying on the generosity and insight of a tremendous number of individuals. I'm fortunate to be surrounded by so many talented (and patient) friends and colleagues. I'd like to thank everyone who contributed to the creation of this book—it would not exist without you.

First off, I'd like to thank Tony Zingale and John Rizzo for having the vision, patience, and belief required to bring this book to fruition and for "encouraging" me when I lost faith. And to my wife, Saira, who on top of running her own business, teaching, serving on boards, and holding down every aspect of our family life somehow manages to find time to support my crazy endeavors.

I'd like to thank everyone who contributed thought leadership, experience, insights, and perspective to the substance of this book including Adam Mertz, Adam Nash, Allison Kaplan, Andrea Bredow, Andy Sernovitz, Andy Wang, Anna-Christina Douglas, Beth Laking, Bill Lanfri, Bill Lynch, Bob Benz, Brace Rennels, Brian Carr, Claire Flanagan, Dave DeWalt, Dave Gutelius, David Cook, Deirdre Walsh, Esteban Kolsky, Gia Lyons, Greg D'Alesandre, Greg Gerik, Ian MacLeod, Jeff Coleman, Jesper Sørensen, Joe Kraus, John Schwiller, John Stepper, Josh Leslie, Justin Fitzhugh, Kathryn Everest, Kevin Mazzola, Lance Riedel, Marc Andreessen, Mark Leslie, Mark Weitzel, Matt Tucker, Nathan Rawlins, Nilofer Merchant, Paula Young, Rajat Paharia, Ray Wang, Ryan Rutan, Scott Johnston, Scott Ross, Simon Levene, Steve Kahl, Tim Albright, and Tim Zonca. You see things before they become obvious to the rest of us. I learned a lot from each and every one of you; I'm excited that others will also benefit from your knowledge.

There are many pitfalls, traps, and mistakes in the publishing journey for a newbie. I had the benefit of being coached by some outstanding authors who took the journey before me. To Andy McAfee, Gianluigi Longinotti-Buitoni, Andy Sernovitz, Paul Greenberg, Rajat Paharia, Hunter Muller, and Melissa Barker: thanks for setting my expectations and teaching me that there are many things to think about other than just the publisher.

I'd like to thank everyone who helped with some aspect of the creation process: Jason Zeiber for an incredible cover. Lorena Guerra for all of her work on the visuals. Sydney Sloan, Megan Moxley, Robert Pollie, and John McCracken for helping to pull together and get approval for some amazing case studies. Suzame Tong for ensuring we got the resources we needed and, along with Christelle Flahaux, Amanda Pires, and Jason Khoury, for helping to get the word out to the world and present the book in its best light. Sarah Weatherhead and Bill Pierznik who translated legalese and helped keep me out of trouble.

Enormous thanks go to Diana Reynolds Roome, our esteemed editor. You efficiently transformed a document into a polished manuscript. Unbelievably, we never wore you down.

For lending me the weight of their reputations and endorsing the book, I'd like to thank Jon Bidwell, HK Dunston, Aaron Levie, Ray Wang, Andy McAfee, Paul Greenberg, Nilofer Merchant, Debby Hopkins, Rob Koplowitz, Scott Tweedy, Mark Yolton, and Tony Zingale. To have your public support is flattering beyond words. So simply, thank you.

Thanks to the entire McGraw-Hill Business team for all of their hard work making this book a reality. I'd especially like to thank Stephanie Frerich for believing in the book and making the case to publish it and Knox Huston for being a fantastic partner through the process.

Lastly, I'd like to thank my partner in crime, Sara Leslie. I'm not sure either of us knew the enormity of what we were taking on when we started this project, although I do credit her with trying to talk me out of it. Thank you for the endless hours of writing, rewriting, rewriting, rewriting, researching, cat herding, project management, Chris management, and tenacious follow-through. I know you are smart enough to never want to write a book with me again, but if I ever wrote one there is no one else I would want on the project!

Sara Gaviser Leslie:

In addition to the great partners Chris noted above, I'd like to thank all of my family and especially my little guys: Devin, Sammy, and Theo. Thank you for your unwavering support. Most importantly, to my husband, Josh, you have patience beyond belief. You kept me going and always pointed me toward the light at the end of the tunnel, even when it was incredibly hard to see!

Lisa Solomon, Jennifer Aaker, Sarah Milstein, Joanna Strober, and Lyn Denend: your guidance on the writing and publishing process was invaluable. Allison Kaplan, Amy Abrams, Bethany Coates, Charlotte Zdanowski, Dawn Wells Nadeau, Debbie Winick, Hannah Park, Helen Plewman, Kim Jabal, Lisa Sweeney, Sharon Leslie, Stacy Goldman, and Susannah Shimkus, the 738 crew, and, of course, my 5:50 a.m. team: you encouraged me always and ceaselessly listened to me when the deadline seemed to move further and further into the future.

Finally, this project would never have come to fruition without the humor, intellect, foresight, optimism, and diplomacy of Chris Morace. I feel very fortunate to have had an excellent partner—and friend—in this process. You always believed we could do this. You were right.

CHAPTER 1

DISRUPTION IN THE ENTERPRISE

WHAT, WHY, AND THE CHOICES COMPANIES MUST MAKE

NEW TECHNOLOGIES SPUR THE PACE OF CHANGE

The inventions that humankind has hatched just during the past five years are appearing exponentially faster than developments in the last 50 years or in any period since the beginning of the Industrial Age. During the Stone Age (ended between 4500 and 2000 BCE), hunter-gatherers and, later, farmers, developed tools to help them do their jobs—stone cutting tools and arrowheads among other simple inventions. Later, in the Bronze Age (ended around 1200 BCE), and then the Iron Age (ended around 200 CE), humans invented the catapult, gunpowder, the clock, and the wheel. These machines were monumental to human progress, but they are nothing compared to today's technological innovations. In mere years or even over months, humans are launching multiple inventions, many of which are more revolutionary than those the people of the Stone Age hatched over a period of 3.4 million years.[1]

Futurist Raymond Kurzweil, in his book *The Singularity Is Near*, highlights the evolution of communications technologies as proof that the speed of technology adoption is rapidly accelerating:

> A half millennium ago, the product of a paradigm shift such as the printing press took about a century to be widely deployed. Today, the products of major paradigm shifts, such as cell phones and the World Wide Web, are widely adopted in only a few years' time.[2]

Technological Innovation: The Industrial Age and Rapid Development

The Industrial Revolution took machinery up several notches. Individuals who lived through this period—beginning around 1700—saw magic everywhere. Who could have imagined the ability of anesthesia to blunt pain during a medical procedure, the detail of a photograph to help you remember a scene exactly as it was, the power of a telegraph to send a message across the country, or the speed at which a spinning jenny could turn wool into yarn?

Some of the most remarkable inventions were in the area of transportation. Steam-powered trains and ships, automobiles, and electrical messaging devices replaced horse-based travel, saved hundreds of man-hours, and gave people the ability to interact with others far beyond their immediate environments.

Communications technologies offer the best evidence that the pace of change is increasing. For thousands, if not millions, of years, humans used messengers and signal fires to communicate over long distances. The only ways to convey information were face-to-face or with visual signals. Even in 1845, it took President James K. Polk six months to get a message from Washington, D.C., to California.

The telegraph quickly displaced the Pony Express in 1861 and made it possible to send and receive messages almost instantaneously.[3] By separating information into short messages, humans could communicate more quickly. Shortly thereafter, in 1876, Alexander Graham Bell invented the telephone transmitting not just data but also voice. Initially, the phone was a very expensive tool. As it became more affordable in the 1900s—and had higher performance—large portions of the population were able to access the phone. It was no longer a tool of governments, corporations, and the wealthy alone. Then, digital communication accelerated in the late twentieth century with the facsimile machine, e-mail, mobile phones, SMS messaging (mobile texting), and video chat services like Skype in the early twenty-first century. Compared to how long it took for the telephone to replace foot messengers and U.S. mail, these digital developments occurred over an extremely compressed time frame.

Rapid innovation is becoming the norm. If Kurzweil is correct about the accelerating pace of change, we should prepare for a wild ride:

> [W]e won't experience one hundred years of technological advance in the twenty-first century; we will witness on the order of twenty thousand years of progress (again, when measured by *today's* rate of progress), or about one thousand times greater than what was achieved in the twentieth century.[4]

Initially, connecting to the Internet involved buying a modem and hooking that up to a computer; now the modem is inside many devices such as tablets and e-readers. Business travelers who needed to connect to their company's network from a hotel room struggled to disconnect the hotel phone, find a toll-free access number from the data carrier (lest they rack up a double or triple digit phone bill), and endured multiple dropped calls before finally reaching their company files and e-mails. Now, we expect technology to be easy to use and readily available from anywhere. When an airplane doesn't have Wi-Fi service, we see it as an injustice!

The pace of change is accelerating at a rate that the world has never before experienced, yet it's happening so quickly it almost goes unnoticed. Kurzweil notes, "Exponential growth is deceptive. It starts out almost imperceptibly and then explodes with unexpected fury—unexpected, that is, if one does not take care to follow its trajectory."[5]

THE PACE OF CHANGE DISRUPTS
THE STATUS QUO

The End of Command and Control Warfare and Management

Once, a few large players dominated all operations, attacks, and, of course, wars. They made periodic moves that required well-researched and coordinated responses. Then, real threats began to materialize from almost anywhere in the world with very little notice. Following the collapse of the Soviet Union and the rise of smaller terror organizations not directly tied to nation-states, the U.S. Military restructured to better respond to changing power structures. It shifted dramatically toward an investment in Special Forces. The military gives these small teams extensive training, broad access to information and communication technologies, and empowers them with decision making within a mission-based framework.

In the business world, too, advanced planning and coordinated responses are becoming outdated behaviors. New communications technologies enable companies to get information to customers faster, understand customer behavior, and analyze how partners behave. Instead of sending a memo through interoffice mail and waiting days for a response, workers send an e-mail and hear back in a minute. They then have no choice but to act on this new information. A mass market retailer, for instance, can no longer wait for each individual store to count inventory to know which products are selling. Instead, it must invest in sophisticated point-of-sale systems to send transaction information directly to headquarters. That generates a new challenge that must be responded to without delay. The company must reroute inventory or change promotions with almost no advance planning.

Whereas the Industrial Age was about command and control and hierarchical structures, computational global networks dominate everything and everyone in the Information Age.[6] Distributed computational global networks set free the flow of data and information. They enable people to communicate at near zero cost. Data flows rapidly so members of the network learn about new developments quickly. As soon as they learn of them, they must act on them.

Thus the speed of business accelerates!

Businesses Run the Red Queen's Race

Alice, the main character in Lewis Carroll's *Through the Looking-Glass*, experienced this same relentless acceleration on her adventure. One character she encountered, the Red Queen, challenges Alice to a race across a chessboard. In the Red Queen's race, Alice finds that she must run faster and faster only to stay in the same place. Frustrated and panting, Alice turns to the Queen and says, "In our country, you'd generally get to somewhere else—if you run very fast for a long time." To this the Red Queen responds, "A slow sort of country! Now, here, you see, it takes all the running you can do, to keep in the same place. If you want to go somewhere else, you must run at least twice as fast as that!"[7]

Today's businesses are in a similar predicament; they're running twice as fast but making little progress. It's like an accelerating treadmill with an equally elusive finish line. When business processes hit the limits of their speed, devices like smartphones seek to make workers more productive, but only at the expense of their evenings, weekends, and vacations.

Command and control was once the dominant management style in the enterprise. But in an environment of fast-flowing information, this approach doesn't work. Instead, like militaries that replace large platoons with special forces teams, firms need adaptive organizational models that are responsive to rapid shifts in product innovations, customer tastes, or regulatory environments.

When companies can't adapt to a new environment and an accelerating pace of change, they bend or break. An enterprise is like a machine that runs a large set of processes. As change occurs more frequently, enterprises have to respond to these changes more quickly. This requires agility and adaptability. When you increase the rate of processes, exceptions to the standard process also increase. You get someone to handle exceptions and that person becomes the new bottleneck. The company cannot complete the process fast enough.

Push Out Now, Correct Later

Technology is transforming media perhaps more than any other industry; news breaks first on Twitter, and journalists and police identify suspects through Facebook photos. As Allison Kaplan, senior editor at *Mpls. St. Paul Magazine* explains:

> Newspaper, magazine, and TV reporters feel pressure to produce more news faster. We're still doing the "traditional" work, whether that's in print or on camera, but now we have all of the other channels to constantly feed—blogs, social media (Foursquare, Instagram, Facebook, Twitter, Pinterest, and YouTube) e-newsletters, apps, and more. The rapid growth and immediacy of these channels and the constant need to feed them is eroding a basic tenet of journalism: fact checking. The new philosophy is push it out now, correct it later. We saw this in December 2012 as the horrors in the Newtown, Connecticut, shootings unfolded.[8]

Agile software development is gaining popularity because it enables developers to continually validate their ideas through an iterative and flexible process. While the interim product might not be perfect, this "put it out, correct it later" is an overriding theme of agile. Shorter, iterative loops are replacing long planning cycles.

Sheryl Sandberg, COO of Facebook, explains how Facebook, among other technology companies, has adopted the lean approach that Eric Ries details in his book, *The Lean Start-up: How Today's Entrepreneurs Use Continuous Innovation to Create Radically Successful Businesses*:

> Traditionally, companies have depended on elaborate business plans and in-depth tests to put out a "perfect" product. Ries advocates that for tech, a better way to perfect a product is to introduce it to the market and get customers using it and giving feedback, so you can learn and then iterate. (Facebook figured out this approach long ago. We even have posters all over our buildings that remind people, "Stay Focused & Keep Shipping.")[9]

Business processes—not just software development—must also become agile. In fact, the ability to adapt is becoming more important than any other quality, even speed. The environment is changing so quickly that even if you plan, you find that by the time you follow through on your plan, the environment has changed.

How can technology support firms' need for adaptability? In the past, technology helped enterprises manage and automate processes. Today, this software is incompatible with a constantly evolving environment. Jesper Sørensen, a professor of organizational behavior at Stanford Graduate School of Business, explains that much of the technology currently installed in the enterprise has reached its limits:

> Systems like ERP, supply chain management, and Six Sigma are
> designed to enable companies to get better at the things they
> already know how to do. They reduce inefficiency in the flow
> of information about known processes and known procedures.
> The downside of these systems is that they encode a particular
> understanding of a strategy and operational routines. It's
> difficult to fit new processes, new programs, and new businesses
> into an existing system.[10]

In other words, these systems worked until something in the environment changed. When a problem arises with a product, customer tastes change, or competitors emerge, a company's ability to react quickly becomes more important than consistency. In a dynamic environment, mechanization is the wrong approach; the enterprise is all engine and no steering. When you're drag racing, all you need is to go fast. But any time you want to turn, steering becomes critical. Companies have spent millions of dollars for information technology, yet they can't navigate a rapidly changing environment.

Innovation has overtaken companies' ability to react quickly.

Enterprises Need New Tools to Process New Information

In distributed organizations, a major challenge is getting all employees the right information they need to make good decisions. Enterprises are becoming larger, faster paced, organic organizations, and company information is flowing more freely both inside and outside the enterprise. Companies must monitor and react to this information.

But enterprises don't have the resources to support this kind of communication, so they optimize around constraints. They find a way to amplify their strengths and mitigate their weaknesses and punt or delay on anything that they don't know how to manage. They add resources around a problem when they can't solve the problem. They create a queue and watch customers line up for help.

Though enterprises can quickly transport information and shrink the information loop—the time and effort to get information from one person to another—we haven't seen the same acceleration and adjustments in human information processing. As marketing guru Seth Godin suggests, "We don't need people to write down the answer, information is abundant. We need help processing things, help finding surprise and insight. ..."[11]

The problem is, current tools can't process information quickly enough.

When enterprises can't process information quickly and easily, they can't respond to threats like shifts in product or service needs, customer tastes, technology and socioeconomic factors; opportunities available from internal competencies; or potential opportunities with partners or mergers/acquisitions.

As Sørensen explains:

> Enterprises tend to lack the systems to support communication
> around new ideas and information discovery. Getting ideas to take
> hold depends on finding the right audience. If I'm working in an
> organization and come up with a new idea, I want to share it; I want
> to tell other people about it and get them to support it. I'm going to
> talk to the first person I run into in the hallway and tell them about
> my idea. If that person isn't interested or doesn't think it is a good
> idea, the idea dies. The only way to keep the idea moving is to be
> very convincing or continually search for the right audience.[12]

Systems like CRM and ERP don't capture the conversations that don't fit anywhere; the conversations that take place on the phone, over e-mail, or even in person. Companies don't have an easy way to make these conversations available to a wider audience or even have a record of them for the future. Andy Sernovitz, author of *Word of Mouth Marketing: How Smart Companies Get People Talking*, explains it this way:

Customer relationship management systems took customer data formally stored in silos and made that data accessible across an organization. But what about the conversations that keep people in organizations aware of what's happening? That describe what do to in exceptional cases? That clarify procedures when automation isn't enough?

What we lack, Sernovitz suggests is a "database of conversations."[13]

The Goliaths of the world experience this happening. They hear about up-and-coming players, they know customers are choosing competitors' products over theirs, but they can't efficiently process the information they are gathering both internally and externally. When they finally do process this information, they are unable react and refocus their business on the threat quickly enough to strike back at new competitors.

Established firms are losing revenue and market share. They're not able to understand, coordinate, and take advantage of new tools quickly enough to remain competitive. Just when they've gotten used to one system, a new one arises. Innovation cycles are shrinking. As John Doerr, a partner at venture capital firm Kleiner Perkins Caufield & Byers, remarked, "Today, these two products at Apple [holds up an iPhone and an iPad mini] that didn't exist a few years ago are now $100 billion a year of very profitable revenue."[14]

The world has never felt so in flux.

The information systems that we've put in place over the last 200 years are failing us in the face of unprecedented change. But it isn't just the systems. It's the processes as well. It is the way we manage our organizations. It's the rhythms of the way we process information, communicate our decisions, and review our performance. The models still being used today have been in place for centuries. Annual planning, semiannual reviews, quarterly all hands—all speak to a pace and cadence of times past.

Whether in a crisis or the course of regular business, companies see their businesses failing even with sophisticated, custom technology. They say, "I've mechanized my business—why isn't it responsive?" They've laid down the railroad tracks but are struggling to get the train to go somewhere else, somewhere the tracks don't reach. No wonder they're puzzled and frustrated! Enterprises might be getting the results they intended—predictable and repetitive outcomes. But when the desired outcomes, competitors, customer needs, and other aspects of the operating environment change, businesses start to break.

The same technologies that made it possible for companies to automate processes, gain more control of their business, and keep production on track instead begin to hinder an enterprise's ability to be agile and adapt to a changing environment. Companies struggle to stay in control. They lack early warning systems to notify them when it's time to evolve their businesses. They are under so much pressure to compete that they don't feel they have the time to determine in which direction to go. So they manage by trying to just move with the speed of the market. The changes that they must make pile up, but they don't have the capacity to address these shifts.

Then, eventually, they lose control.

New Tools and Systems Evolve—Bringing Communications Full Circle

So this is the impetus: The pressures of the rapid pace of change and technology introductions propel the new organization models and communication technologies that allow the enterprise to adapt to a changing market.

Here's a fascinating fact. We are coming full circle in terms of the quality of communication between individuals and groups. During the Industrial Age, hierarchical organizations spread employees further apart and, not surprisingly, quality and quantity of interaction suffered. Today's technologies—social, mobile, cloud, and big data—actually bring people closer together. They enable enterprises, partners, customers, and even competitors to interact in global computational and communication networks. These global computational networks are similar to agrarian tribal networks, where proximity of all members led to high-quality communication.

But unlike these clans and families, new technologies can allow individuals to overcome limits of physical space and time in communication; we get high-quality interaction over great distances.

The nervous system that languished during the Industrial Age—specifically, direct connectivity between people and entities—is back.

And that means the infrastructure for social networks is now in place.

TECHNOLOGY READINESS EQUALS LONGEVITY

A firm's ability to harness new technology is the key to its longevity. It is enabling the Davids to compete effectively with—if not quite kill—the Goliaths. In fact, software and technological superiority are becoming the main triggers for disruption. As Marc Andreessen suggests,

> More and more major businesses and industries are being run on software and delivered as online services—from movies to agriculture to national defense. Many of the winners are Silicon Valley–style entrepreneurial technology companies that are invading and overturning established industry structures. Over the next 10 years, I expect many more industries to be disrupted by software, with new world-beating Silicon Valley companies doing the disruption in more cases than not.[15]
>
> [I]n many industries, new software ideas will result in the rise of new Silicon Valley-style start-ups that invade existing industries with impunity. Over the next 10 years, the battles between incumbents and software-powered insurgents will be epic.

Dion Hinchcliffe, an information technology expert, says technology isn't just reshaping business, it is causing an earthquake:

> It's more like it's leaving the traditional business world behind. There are a number of root causes: The blistering pace of external innovation, the divergent path the consumer world has taken from enterprise IT, and the throughput limitations of top-down adoption.[16]

Start-ups Have No Baggage

The established and entrenched companies of today are playing defense as they try to keep up with the pace of change. Companies that were once just annoying ankle biters are now serious threats. They can implement new technologies quickly, change course with little notice, and compete unencumbered. The start-ups have an even greater ability to take advantage of the land grab for customers, to form strong connections with these customers, and to understand and build new products based on these customers' behavior.

Commercial and Retail Banks and Credit Cards vs. Square

Until recently, if a personal finance and banking start-up wanted to compete with big banks or credit card companies, it seemed improbable it would ever succeed. Consumers were wedded to their credit cards and switching costs were high. Now, these roles are reversed. Companies like PayPal and Square are offering mobile payments, peer-to-peer payments, and incremental billing, shaking up an industry that was originally built for a far simpler world. The entrenched financial services firms struggle to evolve. Their massive infrastructure, interdependent supply chain, and even repetitive processes were once barriers to disruption but are now the very factors that prevent agility and responsiveness.

Mint and Intuit

Intuit was a pioneer of personal finance and small business software—Quicken, TurboTax, and the like. But even Intuit was caught off guard when a young rival, Mint.com, started offering a budget-tracking service that had a more attractive interface than Quicken and used social media to acquire customers. Intuit sent a bullying letter to Mint.com asking it to explain its explosive growth. As Brad Smith, Intuit's CEO, later apologetically recalled, "It looked like Goliath picking on David." Even though Intuit had launched an online version of its Quicken software, it couldn't match Mint's simple—and free—product. Eventually, in 2009, Intuit purchased Mint.com.[17]

Electronic Arts and Zynga

Electronic Arts, an electronic games publisher founded in 1982, was once the leading game developer, licensing sports team names and movie titles to produce games for video consoles. Zynga, the mobile game company that debuted in 2007, is the main party responsible for Electronic Arts posting losses in two-thirds of its fiscal quarters from June 2005 to December 2012. Zynga determined that consumer convenience and social networking were the most important features it could offer in a gaming platform. Players preferred to battle against friends on mobile phones rather than sit in their basements with a game console. The "deluxe model" of game development is a thing of the past, Zynga believes, and the market favors data-driven online games.

Zynga's approach leverages technology to build games. Instead of following the old movie production model of creating a massive product and dropping it on the market, Zynga prioritizes the ability to understand real-time user information and constantly make incremental changes to games. It develops games for a tenth of the cost of Electronic Arts's games but earns double the return on investment. Electronic Arts CEO John Riccitiello recognizes the company has been late to the mobile and social gaming world and admitted, "The other guys have lapped us three times." Zynga, on the other hand, doesn't even think of itself as a gaming company. Rather, it sees itself as a data company that makes games addictive—and makes it easy to find other game addicts to play with anywhere, anytime.[18]

Established Companies Struggle to Integrate New Technology

Smaller start-up companies gain power over the more established firms because they lack baggage, both in terms of technical infrastructure and work processes. This baggage they lack was once seen as powerful, even essential assets: established processes; a large employee population; physical offices; strategic investments; property, plant, and equipment; and predictable revenue streams and customers. In a rapidly changing environment, these assets that once put a company at an advantage now become disadvantages. Start-ups can implement new technology without the burden of integrating legacy systems. And, they can get these important systems up and running for a fraction of what it cost those who came before them.

The Trouble with an Installed Base

Dominic Orr of Aruba Networks claims that speed is the biggest advantage that start-up companies can claim. They must have both speed of execution and speed of innovation:

> I remember when I first entered the industry there was a popular saying that the reason God could create heaven and earth in seven days was because he did not have an installed base. So the big company has this legacy of stuff that they have to sell, and they have a certain expectation of what they should avoid, and what brand to project and so on. They have to stay the course.[19]
>
> What we're really relying on for the start-up is the ability to go full speed ahead without the burden of the installed base.

Sony Electronics and Apple's iPod

The story of disruption in consumer electronics has evolved over the past 12 years. Sony, once the consumer electronics giant, provided one of the greatest devices in personal electronics. When it first introduced the Walkman, it gave individuals the power to take their music with them anywhere. It was the end to large stereos and portable, but heavy, boom boxes. Sony continually introduced a smaller and smaller Walkman until, eventually, the machine was only slightly bigger than the tape itself.

Following the success of the Walkman, Sony introduced the Discman, the first portable compact disc player. Consumers saw compact discs as the next music standard; they had higher-quality audio and were easily portable in a collection. Then Sony moved into CDs to capitalize on this evolution. The motivation wasn't primarily to create a better customer experience. Supporting the Discman rather than the Walkman allowed the company to increase margins and sell discs to those customers who had previously purchased cassette tapes. CDs were sexy and had better sound quality than cassettes; music companies could charge a premium price.

Sony sat at the pinnacle of the consumer electronics world in the 1980s and mid-1990s. But quickly, market disrupters—most notably, Apple—used technology to usurp Sony as the market's leader. Even before Apple introduced the iPod, other MP3 players hit the market with their versions including the Diamond RIO, I2Go, and Audio Highway Listen Up. These devices could play digital files, but none disrupted the music world. Users struggled with the devices' size, storage capacity, and user interface. The lack of music that listeners could download legally also hindered widespread adoption.

The iPod, however, was a game-changing device: 1,000 songs in your pocket! Apple figured out that people wanted a product that was easy to use, and efficiently developed a device that could hold lots of songs with a small form factor. Apple also recognized that the channels of distribution were as important, if not more important than the product itself. Steve Jobs saw a link between media producers and devices. He knew that if people couldn't get media easily and legally, the product would not succeed. So, along with a great device, Apple offered a simple way to acquire music through the iTunes Store. Beyond 1,000 songs in your pocket, Apple knew it could disrupt the consumer electronics industry further. It traumatically displaced the digital camera, phone, portable music device, and personal digital assistant—clobbering them all at once with the iPhone.

Along with great technology, Apple offered a superior user experience and enabled users to manage their own music and listening experience. As Sohrab Vossoughi, founder, president, and chief creative director of design firm Ziba, explains:

> Apple's iPhone ... only comes in one current model and two colors, yet it's tremendously customizable. With so much of the experience coming from the software, not the hardware, consumers aren't using a product designed for them; it was designed by them. ... Every time they install an app or download a song, users are getting a customized experience with an emotional impact on par with the one-time purchase of a product.[20]

Sony didn't lose out to Apple because its products were technolog-
ically faulty; Sony had a well-deserved reputation for excellence.
The real reason Sony ceded control of the consumer electronics
to Apple was because Sony couldn't leverage new technology and
new business models fast enough. It assumed product development and engagement ended when its product hit the customer's
hands. Apple had a more modern view of technology. To Apple,
the customer's purchase was only the beginning of product development. Apple designed a vertically integrated system where it
manufactured the music store, player, and jukebox software for the
computer in-house. By owning this end-to-end platform, Apple
circumvented Sony's ability to respond. Apple made it possible
for consumers to have their music with them instantly, anywhere,
anytime.

Fast Fashion vs. Department Stores

It used to be that customers looked to the stores or magazines
to find out the latest trends. Department and specialty stores
followed long-range planning calendars. They built their eco-
systems around the fall fashion launch and three additional collections. All merchandise came in at one time, mid-August, to
prepare the store for back-to-school shopping. If stores missed a
trend, they missed sales because it took them 90 days to produce
merchandise.

This model worked until the fast fashion powerhouses—
Forever 21, Sweden's H&M, Japan's Uniqlo, and Spain's Zara—
entered their territory. They captured street fashion trends and
used systems that combine short production and distribution
times to match supply with demand and trendy product design.

By keeping manufacturing local, Zara produces merchandise
within 14 days and takes delivery of new inventory on a daily
basis. Zara's system relies on constant "exchange of information
throughout every part of Zara's supply chain—from customers
to store managers, from store managers to market specialists and
designers, from designers to production staff, from buyers to subcontractors, from warehouse managers to distributors."[21]

Zara also trains employees to draw out comments from customers. When customers tell store employees that they prefer

no zippers on their pants or they like the rounded collar on the blouse, the sales staff gives this information to store managers who then report it to headquarters. At headquarters, the team of in-house designers quickly develops new designs based on this feedback and sends them to Zara's factories where they are manufactured into new, hot items.[22]

Because Zara must continually communicate on trends in order to maintain an inventory of the most current merchandise, Zara designed its business—everything from the organization, operational procedures, performance measures, and office layouts—to facilitate easy information transfer.[23] Now, when trend spotters post on blogs and other social media sites, fast fashion retailers like Zara can respond quickly.

Fast fashion can mean disposable fashion to many, but rising sales demonstrate success. Annual revenues for fast-fashion retailers Forever 21, Uniqlo, H&M, and Zara increased an average of 18 percent from 2006 to 2010, according to a report called *Fashion NYC 2020*. During the same period, specialty retailers like Aéropostale and Gap saw sales rise only 2 percent.[24] Fast-fashion retailers are openings stores while department stores and specialty retailers like the Gap are shutting outlets.

In order to capture micro trends and more fickle customers, department and specialty stores have begun to change their collections 10 times a year or more. Even high-end brands like Prada and Louis Vuitton have moved from two collections a year to four or six. They are hoping to be as successful as the fast fashion retailers at driving traffic and sales. Unlike these fast fashion retailers, however, department stores are encumbered by legacy IT systems and tired real estate.

Zara controls the supply chain by bucking the trend and not subcontracting all manufacturing to Asia. It created a partner network of more than 300 small shops that can handle finishing work. While these changes fly counter to most clothing manufacturing trends, what really propels Zara is technology. The company has 14 highly automated Spanish factories with robotic workers and leverages just-in-time manufacturing to develop and bring new products to stores with unprecedented speed. Zara addresses market demands before retailers with traditional models can possibly respond. Speed and flexibility have enabled Zara's parent, the Spanish firm Inditex SA, to become the world's largest clothing retailer.[25]

U.S. Mail and FedEx

FedEx revolutionized a business-to-business industry. The company used logistical software and new scanning to appear out of nowhere and become a leader in package delivery. It created a nationwide clearinghouse for packages and launched an integrated system of trucks and planes in order to give the level of service customers demanded. As Frederick Smith, FedEx's founder, explains:

> We had to use information technology to an extent that had never been done before. We had to basically create a whole industry to do that. It wasn't just the tracking system. We had to develop a completely new printing methodology.
>
> And no one had ever contemplated building a handheld computer that was this small [holds his hands close together] and then communicated that information on a real-time basis. We had to assemble all these radio frequencies and put the equipment in the truck. When we developed this tracking system, it meant you could actually keep up, for the first time ever, with inventory that was moving as well as inventory that was stationary.[26]

Even when the U.S. Postal Service began offering overnight delivery, FedEx's technology was so far ahead that the little white trucks never stood a chance of regaining market share. In the third quarter of 2012, the USPS registered a $15.9 billion loss for the year and was on the verge of bankruptcy.

The companies that can't start with a clean slate must figure what new solutions to implement first. They are trying to move forward, but they are still shackled by legacy enterprise software—ERP, CRM, knowledge management, intranet, etc. Economists suggest companies should "ignore sunk costs," but it's not only technology investments that companies must overcome. Enterprise IT architecture is so complicated today that it's not even clear where to begin.

THE REINFORCING LOOP OF TECHNOLOGY INNOVATION

Existing technologies don't just fail to meet the needs of today's enterprises; they actually prevent established enterprises from harnessing those technologies that would help them manage the pace of change. Enterprises and young upstarts fight for control over consumer and business dollars. It's not those that own the land or resources who control outcomes. In an environment that is changing quickly, flexibility and youth are assets. Companies that haven't made significant infrastructure investments and don't have well-honed processes have an advantage over those companies with established businesses. These younger firms can switch course more quickly and easily without disruption. As they become more adept at managing new technology, they move even further ahead of the established firms. The ability to master and leverage new technologies becomes a reinforcing loop that favors younger, more agile firms.

Corporate Longevity Decreases

Look no further than the makeup of the S&P 500 for evidence as to how difficult it is for companies to manage an accelerating pace of change and stay relevant for the long term. Of the 500 companies originally making up the S&P 500[27] in 1957, only 74 remained on the list through 1997. Of those 74, only 12 outperformed the S&P over the 1957–1998 period.[28]

According to McKinsey & Company consultants Richard Foster and Sarah Kaplan:

> In the '20s and '30s the turnover rate in the S&P 90 averaged about 1.5 percent per year. A company that was added to the S&P 90 at that time could expect to remain on the list, on average, for more than 65 years. Corporations of the '20s and '30s focused on staying in business. They transformed raw materials into final products and operated at great scale and controlled their costs carefully. Vertical integration meant they were protected from all but incremental change.

Corporate sustainability is eroding at an ever-increasing rate. By 1998 the turnover rate on the S&P 500 was close to 10 percent, implying an average lifetime on the list of 10 years, far below the 65 years of the 1920s and 1930s. By 2020, 75 percent of the companies in the S&P will be companies that weren't widely recognized in 2001.[29]

The Normal Curve Shifts

Technology is integral to achievement and permanency, yet keeping up with technological changes is hard for companies, especially established firms. Foster and Kaplan explain, "It is among the relatively new entrants to the economy—for example, Intel, Amgen and Cisco—where one finds superior performance, at least for a time."[30] With the introduction of each new technology, the pace of work accelerates.

The companies that can harness the newest technologies gain an incremental advantage over their competition—and survive.

A business's offerings can sit, hypothetically, on a curve. When the pace of change increases, one by one, companies incorporate new features or offer new products. This phenomenon is shown in Figure 1.1. The first medical supply company that offered electronic data interchange to hospitals gained market share from its laggard competitors. The first pharmacy that offered online refills experienced a flood of new patients, at least until all other pharmacies offered the same convenient service.

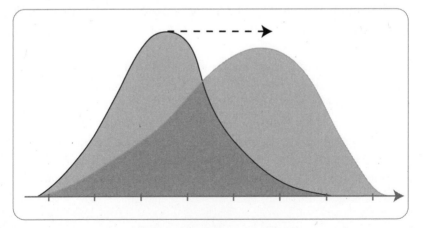

FIGURE 1.1. The Normal Curve Shifts

Each innovator pushes the rest of the companies in an industry forward, shifting the curve to the right, until they slow down from increasing bottlenecks—or break.

DISRUPTION PUTS COMPANIES AT A CROSSROADS

Each successive wave of innovation and disruption happens faster and more powerfully. Today, cloud, mobile, social, and big data aren't successive waves but, instead, are hitting enterprises simultaneously like a tidal wave. These technologies are big and powerful as the Internet was in the 1990s. However, because the pace of change is so fast, companies have even less time to evolve their business models.

Right now we are at the crossroads. Most enterprises need to understand the new technologies and reimagine their businesses with those technologies. But an increasing pace of change and shortening development cycles give innovators many opportunities to disrupt a previous model. The companies that don't innovate fast enough, of course, run the risk of being disrupted. Though they may not realize it, companies have a choice to make. Most firms choose (or default to) the course they are on—a choice that often leads to disappearance. Kodak, Intel, and Microsoft are just three such companies that opted to continue the course rather than innovate.

Staying where you are, safe though it seems, can be riskier than the riskiest change of course.

Kodak Asks, "What Digital Camera?"

Kodak, once the marquee name in photography, had ample warning but failed to grasp the power of innovative technologies. The company continued to move forward with film photography even as digital photography gained ground. When Steven J. Sasson, an electrical engineer who invented the first digital camera at Eastman Kodak in the 1970s, showed his prototype digital camera to Kodak management, he recalls that they didn't take him seriously:

> My prototype was big as a toaster, but the technical people loved it. But it was filmless photography, so management's reaction was, "that's cute—but don't tell anyone about it."[31]

Kodak, even after getting a vision of the future, dismissed an early opportunity to innovate and take a leading position in digital photography. Later, when Sony introduced the first electronic camera in 1981, Kodak took notice and conducted market research into digital photography. Kodak concluded that digital did have the potential to replace film, but that it wouldn't happen for at least 10 years.

In 1986, Kodak developed a megapixel camera. Vince Barabba, a former Kodak executive, believed that this milestone would signal a turning point in digital photography. Unfortunately, the impact of this invention wasn't strong enough to change the company's strategy. Kodak floundered again when it chose to appoint Kay Whitmore, a chemical engineer, as CEO rather than Phil Samper who had a "deep appreciation for digital technology."[32] Whitmore cut research and development at Kodak instead of investing in digital photography. According to George Fischer, who led Kodak from 1993 to 1999, Kodak didn't seriously consider digital as the company's future:

> It was a high-cost manufacturer, with a bloated staff and a sleepy culture that was slow to make decisions. And it regarded digital photography as the enemy, an evil juggernaut that would kill the chemical-based film and paper business that had fueled Kodak's sales and profits for decades.[33]

Kodak declared bankruptcy in 2012.

Intel: Banking on the PC

Intel processors were such an integral part of Windows computing that most PCs were generically referred to as "Wintel" machines. In 2000, Intel had an 80 percent share of the total number of

CPUs shipped. By device, 96 percent of the total CPUs produced by all chipmakers went to PCs, 3 percent went to servers, and less than 1 percent supported mobile device CPUs. By 2011, mobile devices had changed the landscape: 61 percent of the total number of CPUs shipped went to mobile devices. Intel hadn't focused on this channel, however, and its share of total CPUs shipped fell to under 30 percent.[34]

Mobile devices rely more heavily on technology licensed from U.K.–based ARM holdings. Intel actually had the chance to embrace ARM and emphasize the mobile device market but chose to continue to develop its own ×86 processing technology instead. Specifically, in 2006, Intel's CEO Paul Otellini chose to sell off an unprofitable Intel business that used ARM designs. He believed Intel would eventually be able to offer the same kind of energy conserving processor with ×86 technology.[35]

Qualcomm, in contrast, chose to license ARM. And what happened? Qualcomm edged Intel out, becoming the most valuable semiconductor company by market capitalization. Here is proof that making mobile a priority above all other initiatives would have been the right choice for Intel. As the *Wall Street Journal* reported, Otellini's surprise exit "underscores how quickly and decisively the landscape has changed for Intel, which with software partner Microsoft Corporation once dictated key technical standards and drew much of the profit from the computing industry."[36]

Microsoft: "Apple Has No Chance"

Even after Apple created an elegant and beautiful product, the iPhone, Microsoft believed it lacked widespread appeal. Microsoft CEO Steve Ballmer wrongly equated passion for a product with niche markets. He dismissed the iPhone and assumed Microsoft would transfer its market share in PC software to phones:

> There's no chance that the iPhone is going to get any significant market share. No chance. It's a $500 subsidized item. They may make a lot of money. But if you actually take a look at the 1.3 billion phones that get sold, I'd prefer to have our software in 60% or 70% or 80% of them, than I would to have 2% or 3%, which is what Apple might get.[37]

Ballmer later saw Apple gaining buyers, attention, and accolades, but, even then, failed to recognize that Apple and the iPhone were changing the world:

> [I]t's not like we're at the end of the line of innovation that's going to come in the way people listen to music, watch videos, etc. I'll bet our ads will be less edgy. But my 85-year-old uncle probably will never own an iPod, and I hope we'll get him to own a Zune.[38]

In 2007, Microsoft laughed at the prospects of the iPhone. Business users, claimed Microsoft, would never embrace the iPhone because it lacked a keyboard, which made it "not a very good e-mail machine." Ballmer and Microsoft couldn't see beyond the present day; they couldn't understand that e-mail might not be the killer mobile application of the future. Further, Microsoft ignored the traditional adoption and affordability cycles that accompany new technologies. Ballmer believed consumers wouldn't shell out for the "most expensive phone by far ever in the marketplace,"[39] and failed to recognize that prices would decrease as the device improved.

Reimagined Businesses and Managed Disruption

Not every company stays on the same course, however. Some enterprises can assess the environment and start reimagining their business with new technologies. These companies realize they exist in a rapidly changing world. They know they need to embrace change and transform. To stay relevant, they must constantly reinvent themselves.

If a company wants to survive for the long term, Foster and Kaplan of McKinsey advise that it become a "creator, operator and trader of assets," not simply an efficient operator. They suggest that companies do three specific things: increase the pace of change to the level of the market, expose their decision-making processes to make use of the collective talent of the corporation and its partners (and avoid cultural lock-in), and relax conventional notions of control, but not to the detriment of operations.[40] They must evolve from traditional industrial companies with hierarchical management to computational global networks.

Companies that survive through many market cycles share an ability to leverage their global computational networks. They are able to gather and then assimilate the information around them to evolve their business. Several companies, most notably Apple and Amazon.com, have extended their lives through reimagining their business models.

Apple

Apple's original business model was hardware and software for large devices: printers, desktops, and laptops. The Apple II was one of the first highly successful mass-produced microcomputers, and it launched Apple into business. Nevertheless, the company didn't wait for it to flounder. As Steve Jobs recalled:

> The Apple II was running out of gas. We needed to do something
> else. We were on a mission from God to save Apple. No one
> else thought so but it turned out to be true. We reinvented
> manufacturing. We built the product. We built the automated
> factory. We built a distribution system.[41]

Apple disrupts its own business and puts internal pressure on itself to innovate. It killed the floppy disk by building computers without slots for this storage medium. Similarly, it killed the CD-ROM, hard drive, and ports. When a technology reaches the crest of an adoption cycle, Apple kills it. Apple focuses on satisfying customers rather than squeezing all the revenue out of a product. As James Allworth, coauthor with Clay Christensen of *How Will You Measure Your Life?*, explains:

> When your mission is based around creating customer value,
> around creating great products, cannibalization and disruption
> aren't "bad things" to be avoided. They're things you actually
> strive for—because they let you improve the outcome for your
> customer.[42]

Apple launched products that took advantage of new technologies: cloud (iCloud), mobile (iPhone), social (social customer service and developer forums), big data (Siri, Genius), and became a force that almost no consumer electronics firms could dominate. Most notably, Apple didn't just see these technologies in their own right but recognized how they could come together to create a watershed of innovation.

Amazon

Amazon.com has taken a route of continuous reinvention. When it began, it was an online bookseller. Quickly, Amazon added new categories such as music, hard goods, and clothing. Then it went beyond the traditional e-commerce business and leveraged its infrastructure to offer fulfillment for other e-retailers, publishing services, and web services including off-site data storage, all while continuing to sell traditional books.

The Internet was revolutionary because it provided massive connectivity. It enabled individuals and companies to do things they had never been able to do before, including instantly accessing and processing information. The Internet provided the infrastructure for cloud technologies today. In fact, the Internet was largely an infrastructure play. It was like a new phone network—hence the Internet's moniker: the "information superhighway."

Mobile, cloud, big data analytics, and social are more than infrastructure. They reflect how we behave as people—where we communicate, what we say, what we do, and how we connect to ideas. Because these technologies are intertwined with behavior, the transformational potential and impact on individuals that use them is so much greater than the telephone or even the Internet. They are changing the ways we work. Eventually, people won't go anywhere without their mobile devices; very little of their work or personal life won't be touched by these technologies.

These technologies are gaining sophistication and momentum, and combining in ways that we never imagined. They force us to reimagine how our customers want to experience our products and how employees want to work. The cycles of innovation are short, leaving less time to respond. To keep up with the pace of change, firms must constantly integrate new technology to force innovation rather than waiting for the technology to take over. As

Aaron Levie, CEO and founder of Box.net, suggests, "Continuous delivery and continuous deployment is the only way you can survive today in the enterprise."[43] This kind of work simply is not possible with standard enterprise tools.

Though many firms may feel stuck between the past and the future, it is becoming easier to adopt new technology. Levie explains that organizations can now make more strategic choices around their software purchases. The pace at which firms can adopt new technology is only possible because of the way that software and computing resources are now designed and implemented. "In the past, each new application," Levie explains, "required new infrastructure and new competencies, making organizations wary of new additions to the stack. It was far 'easier' to buy your technology from a select few vendors."[44] Today, enterprise technology buyers are more comfortable with the "mix-and-match approach to enterprise IT, and now managing another mobile app or cloud solution is a far more incremental, trivial exercise." Levie suggests that this new method of application delivery is enabling companies to keep up with the accelerating pace of change:

> [U]nsurprisingly, the cycles of disruption are accelerating. Given increasingly lower barriers to distribution, less conservative buyers, and rapidly changing business demands, we're going to see unprecedented change in enterprise technology moving forward.

Starting from Nothing: An Analog in Urban Development and Corporate Crises

Modernizing European Cities

European cities face their own installed base when they make a decision to modernize roads and other infrastructure. Some have to rebuild to make way for modern transportation, but they can't completely raze buildings. For instance, in Brasov, Romania, the roads are too narrow to accommodate larger vehicles (many can't accommodate even a MINI Cooper). Widening the road is not an option when the street is flanked by apartment buildings and storefronts. The city can choose to take down a building here and there and add some public transportation. But, unfortunately, no guide exists as to how best to approach this problem, and no solution fits every city. Instead, cities must begin where the most advantageous opportunities exist.

Remaking Cities After Disasters

A crisis or disaster, however, can create an opportunity for a city or organization to rebuild and modernize. Seattle is just one of a number of American cities that is built on top of itself. In 1889, the Great Seattle Fire demolished the business district. The day following the fire, the city decided to rebuild on the same land. Urban planners realized Seattle could finally solve its tidal flooding and tidal plumbing reversal issues. As the parts of the city that burned first were those built on tidal plains, the builders filled in the ruins and built new buildings where the old ones had stood.[45]

New Orleans has seen a similar situation, an opportunity for renovation. Hurricane Katrina destroyed many of the public schools, homes, and businesses in the area, but also offered the opportunity for rebirth of a great American city. According to the Brookings Institution:

> The sheer magnitude of a catastrophic disaster literally forces a do-over in nearly all aspects of society and governing. . . . The rebuilders of New Orleans saw this as an opportunity to attack poverty and racial disparities, failing public schools, high crime, a segregated health care system, a struggling economy, and fragile coastal protection (just to name a few).[46]

New Orleans didn't let a good crisis go to waste. It focused on making New Orleans more sustainable and a better place to live and conduct business. In comparison to New Orleans before Katrina, the city now has better evacuation plans, charter schools, community-based primary care centers for low-income patients, an improved criminal justice system, and new local government ethics reforms.

Siemens AG

Peter Löscher took over as Siemens' CEO in 2007 after a bribery scandal that ultimately cost the company $98 billion of annual sales, and $1.6 billion in fines in the United States and Germany alone. Siemens and Löscher used the opportunity to reorganize the company. He was the first outsider and non-German to lead Siemens. Löscher conducted a management-review process that led to the replacement of half of the company's top 100 managers, removed managers that lacked accountability, streamlined the company into three key sectors—energy, health care, and industrial—and later added a fourth: cities and infrastructure. Löscher insisted on increasing growth at the same time as he cleaned house. "The speed of change," Löscher says, "was only possible because we were able to use it at the same moment to reposition the whole company."[47] In 2011, for the first time in company history, Siemens earned three times its cost of capital.[48]

Escaping the Red Queen's Mad Race

Companies have overengineered efficiency and exhausted the notion of working harder. They have hit the outer edge of what's possible—yet the demands from customers and competitors keep increasing. The way work is being approached today is unsustainable. Businesses need to find fundamentally new ways to increase productivity and build value. They need to reimagine themselves as companies of the future and let go of the business ideas conceptualized in the eighteenth century that are setting them up for failure. Survival depends upon breaking out of the Red Queen's race entirely—jumping right off that chessboard and into a game they can actually win.

As Nilofer Merchant, author of *11 Rules for Creating Value in the Social Era* and business innovator, suggests:

> Too many organizations that I advise and have studied hold onto to "today" with a vice grip and hope that when the time comes to evolve, they'll be ready. But, the truth is this: you're going to need to manage the present while you invent the future. Really. You're going to have to let go of ways you've already done things. Of the stuff you already do. Of the way in which you are hyper-optimized to deliver what you already know to deliver. Prepare to shift rapidly from opportunity to opportunity.[49]

Technologies like social, mobile, cloud, and big data seemed to promise a path forward, but technology alone has proved to be insufficient. To date, most companies that have embraced these technologies have failed. Behind the headlines of failure, however, a pattern of striking success has emerged. Hundreds of enterprises have transformed the way they work to take full advantage of social, mobile, cloud, and big data to fundamentally improve critical parts of their businesses in measurable ways. They have reduced costs, boosted productivity, accelerated results, and improved outcomes, putting themselves on a completely new business trajectory.

To succeed, companies must do three things well. First, a company must deeply understand these technologies and the new capabilities they offer. Second, it must make the behavioral changes that enable these capabilities to be incorporated into day-to-day operations at a profound level. Finally, it must know where to start, how to avoid pitfalls, how to maintain progress, and how to measure and communicate success.

The journey is long, but taking the first step is urgent. Beginning in the right part of the business allows workforces to become familiar with this new way of working. They can then apply it to other parts of the business and, ultimately, transform their company. Eventually, they move away from battling that stubborn Red Queen and secure their winning place in the race to the future.

CHAPTER 2

THE TECHNOLOGIES CAUSING UNPRECEDENTED DISRUPTION NOW

Social technology stands at the intersection of three powerful technology trends: mobile, cloud, and big data. Cloud, mobile, and big data are, on their own, revolutionary technologies. When they combine with social in the enterprise, they make it possible to get the right information, to the right people, in context. This is the first step in moving beyond command and control management to creating an environment where everyone in the distributed network can play a role in continuous innovation, where everyone has the means to manage the pace of change in their world.

What follows is a general introduction for each technology. Then, we'll get to the nub and explain how each technology interacts with social technologies in the enterprise.

THE PATH TO CLOUD COMPUTING

Cloud computing is the latest stage in the evolution of computing. This started with on-premise-only computing resources and then continued to application service providers (ASPs), software-as-a-service (SaaS), and, finally, cloud computing. By definition, cloud computing is an IT development, deployment, and delivery model that enables real-time delivery of products, services, and solutions over the Internet.

On-Premise Computing

Until the mid-1990s, enterprises relied on computing resources, software, and data resources that the IT department installed on local machines—desktops, laptops, or mobile devices. When they ran out of storage or performance lagged, IT added more hardware. Remember that?

The problem was that enterprise software implementations were complicated. Installing new software required in-house technology experts (or hired consultants) who could get the software working, then provide administration and backup in case it failed. In the 1990s companies implemented enterprise software to automate business processes including accounting, business intelligence, business process management, customer relationship management, master data management, and enterprise resource planning. Regardless of the specific application, implementations lasted many months or even years. An integrator like CSC, Andersen Consulting, Deloitte & Touche, Coopers & Lybrand, Ernst & Young, KPMG Peat Marwick, and PricewaterhouseCoopers would drop 150 analysts at a company's headquarters who would then move in for the duration of the project. When the consultancy's project was done—often after several months—the company expected to have a system that would provide better information for corporate planning and management and, potentially, increase revenues and reduce costs through greater efficiency.

Application-as-a-Service

ASP was one of the first software deployment solutions that introduced off-premise computing. When a company signed with an ASP, the ASP ran the application for the customer. The ASP set up the application on separate hardware and software in the ASP's data center and then gave the customer access to the application over the Internet.

Consider an enterprise that wanted to run a human resources software suite such as PeopleSoft. It needed to buy a UNIX workstation, install PeopleSoft, make it operational, integrate it with a licensed directory application protocol (LDAP), and hire people to manage and maintain the software. An ASP performed all of these tasks for a fee. In fact, the user experience via an ASP felt no different than accessing an on-premise version.

Cloud

Cloud is a computing platform that the owner can configure and grow to satisfy current needs. Cloud architects use Hadoop, a file system and software framework, to run applications and manage data on large clusters of machines. Hadoop makes these many machines appear as one machine. By providing this system-wide view, it's possible to manage files on multiple disks or separate machines, see utilization, and track active users.

The cloud is a true multitenant environment. In a single tenant system like an ASP, each user or company has its own environment, including its own database. You can think of a single tenant system like living in a single family home. True multitenancy is similar to living in a hotel. Tenants share components like an HVAC system, water, electricity, and security. Individuals have their own space but very fluid walls.

Cloud architects accept that hardware—even customized, high-performance hardware—fails. Instead of buying the most expensive equipment, they take failure as a given and focus on redundancy. Large amounts of data no longer reside on a single machine but are distributed over commodity hardware. If a machine goes down, no data is lost.

Even with commodity hardware, an enterprise can get better performance from a cloud environment than from on-premise software. Further, performance doesn't decline as the network grows. We are used to decay curves: the first users on the system get a fast, reliable network, but as more users come online, performance declines for everyone. Cloud computing doesn't work this way. The network never reaches capacity or slows down with the addition of users. The millionth person gets the same experience as the first one on the system.

Updates and upgrades happen seamlessly. A cloud manager updates everyone on the platform at once. Facebook or LinkedIn users can understand this firsthand; they are completely unaware of the changes that are constantly occurring on the network. They never have to download a security patch or upgrade to a new version.

Cloud systems are also asset light. When hardware does fail, it's easy to swap resources in and out; you can add capacity and memory any time. Low hardware costs mitigate the costs of replication. Further, because the cloud architecture is built to scale, these systems' computing power is limitless.

Scale Advantages for Security

Some enterprises fear that if their data aren't on-site, this opens them up to security risks. We'd argue the opposite. Scale advantages make SaaS more secure than an on-premise application. A company's internal security team might optimize security for 20 different applications, but a vendor running a cloud-based application builds it and runs it for one application only. That vendor builds uptime policies, security, and optimization for many customers and, ultimately, does a better job than an internal IT team because the vendor only has to focus on one application.

Beyond basic security, the vendor can afford to invest in a securities audit, establish provisions for customers to give input, and constantly review security policies and procedures. This level of security is only possible because the vendor can spread the costs over many customers.

When users access an application from anywhere and on any device, this presents security challenges. In choosing SaaS over an on-premise application, an enterprise doesn't require special systems management skills and doesn't have to stay on top of security patches to keep the system up to date. And even when an on-premise and off-premise solution cost the same, the off-premise version is actually less expensive because the vendor provides support and security such as specialist monitoring. These services aren't included in the price of the on-premise version, yet the solution isn't complete without them.

The Pay-as-You-Go Model

One of the most unique and valuable attributes of cloud computing is elasticity—the pay-as-you-go and pay-for-what-you-use models. Instead of a company laying out a sizable sum for the computing power, number of users, or storage it needs, the firm can choose its resource needs on demand. Further, anytime a company adds resources from the cloud, they don't disrupt the existing architecture. From the customer's point of view, they don't need to purchase many machines, hire people to manage them, and keep them up and running. Even multinational firms that have the funds and requirements for many servers on premise will struggle to match the utilization and efficiency of a cloud solution.

Cloud Offerings

The three main cloud offerings are platform-as-a-service (PaaS), infrastructure-as-a-service (IaaS), and software-as-a-service. Users access these resources via a web browser on any mobile device. Since users pay for resources incrementally, they can add resources without initiating a large expense approval:

Infrastructure-as-a-Service: Companies and individuals can buy computing infrastructure—storage, hardware, servers, and networking components—in increments. The vendor provides the infrastructure and the developers manually configure, manage, and update numerous components. Rackspace and Amazon Web Services are two examples of IaaS vendors.

Platform-as-a-Service: PaaS takes IaaS once step further. The vendor provides the underlying infrastructure and an application development platform. The PaaS vendor also furnishes the operating systems, databases, middleware, and up-to-date tools and services. A PaaS vendor configures, optimizes, and continuously updates the environment on the user's behalf and includes automation to help developers deploy, test, and iterate applications. The leading PaaS vendors include OpenStack and Google.

Software-as-a-Service: SaaS is the best-known cloud offering. Rather than installing an application on-site—often through a long and expensive process—companies rent the application. Since SaaS is the main delivery model for the social business software, we go into greater depth on it below.

SaaS introduces a new computing architecture and a subscription-based business model. While ASPs hosted a separate instance for each customer, SaaS providers comingle computing resources and take advantage of scale.

Salesforce.com was poster child for SaaS. Instead of a company installing Siebel on its own computers or accessing it via an ASP, a customer purchased a subscription to Salesforce.com and then Salesforce spun up an instance for the customer immediately. (Spinning up an instance is like making a space for a user on an existing network. In many cases, this involves going to a web page and requesting an application or computing power.) Salesforce.com comingles data in a multitenant system rather than setting up infrastructure, including virtual machines, for each user.

The Cloud as the Social Enabler

Cloud computing makes it easier for people and companies to store and distribute content. It is cloud technology that enables social computing to take off in earnest, explains Ian MacLeod, and industry veteran and technology banker:

> The cloud is the critical enabler in social software. Facebook would not have worked if we all had to download a separate piece of software on our PC or other device and then e-mail photos. The cloud enables us to post content once and be assured it will reach a broad, relevant audience that then has the opportunity to comment and react to that content.[1]

The concept of "social technology"—any technology that facilities social interactions through a communications capability such as the

Internet or a mobile device[2]—was born in the cloud with consumer social applications like MySpace and Facebook. Consumer social never left the cloud. From MySpace to Facebook to LinkedIn, users access all of these services through a browser. What the cloud does is to enable social to scale. If LinkedIn started as a desktop service, no one would have paid attention—what connections could you make with only information on your desktop? In the cloud, LinkedIn can see connections between people and seamlessly (to the user) facilitate these connections.

Simpler Integration

The cloud joins disparate systems without expensive connectors. We take these simple integrations for granted, but until recently, if an organization had a portal and wanted it to work with Siebel, it needed a connector from the vendor. The application owners would specify which data, which application programming interface (API), and which specific users would access the system. Then, an in-house IT or professional services person used custom code to link these two systems together. It wasn't a smooth process, and the results were often spotty. When IT updated Siebel, the connection to the portal broke. When IT updated the portal, the connection to Siebel failed. The whole process—and subsequent maintenance—required lots of engineering, people, and patience.

When enterprises access applications from the cloud, issues around integration disappear. Users can have a single identity that is pervasive across the entire organization and all systems, eliminating the need to log into separate systems.

However, simpler integration alone doesn't create efficient communication. A meeting between two people can be easy to arrange and very efficient. Add three more people and participants can still focus on a common goal or finish a task. But consider a meeting for 1,000 people? How do they listen to each other and share information? Just as Facebook created a way to connect 1,000 people with different relationships in a dynamic, scalable environment, a social business platform serves as the central hub for all relationships and connections in an enterprise and, eventually, between enterprises.

MOBILE TECHNOLOGY
UNTETHERS WORKERS

The model of a knowledge worker sitting in a cube and working on a desktop computer is no longer the dominant work style. Today, employees can be just as active outside of the confines of an office. Cities are putting up wireless networks, Apple and Amazon are adding cellular capabilities in all their devices, and airplanes and trains offer wireless access: "going to work" has a new meaning. The year 2010 was an inflection point for global smartphone and tablet sales as sales of these devices surpassed global PC sales. The trend continues; by 2015, PC sales will likely comprise only one-fifth of device sales.[3] The trend toward mobile computing is so strong that, eventually, the mobile device will replace the desktop computer as the primary technology tool in the enterprise.

The future is about how you get your info from anywhere to anyone.[4] When people are working less on desktop computers and more on mobile devices, social tools must also be mobile. The most obvious example of the social and mobile combination is users accessing a social platform via an iPad or iPhone. But this is only the beginning of mobile social networking. Social technology minimizes the difficulties associated with physical separation. When location and context combine with social technology, users receive more specific, accurate, and useful data.

Increasing Sales with Feedback in Context

In other instances, individuals might be interacting with a social platform through a specific functional application. Showpad, for instance, is a presentation tool that connects to a social business platform. Salespeople use Showpad to give rich presentations—including video, graphics, etc.—on a tablet. Members of an organization's marketing department prepare presentations and then load them to Showpad. When salespeople access these presentations through Showpad, they can be assured that they are using the most recent information.

After a sales representative, let's call her Robin, gives the presentation on Showpad, she can enter comments about the presentation, for instance, "This slide was also useful for #healthcare companies." This feedback goes directly to the social business platform where the marketing team sees it. In response, the marketing team quickly posts the specific slide to the healthcare industry presentation. What's so powerful about social and mobile together is that without either the marketing team or Robin doing any extra work, the marketing department can get a report showing where Robin gave the presentation, what other collateral the salesperson shared, and which slides the potential customer found most valuable.

Robin spends a lot of time on the road calling on customers but not actively reaching out to her team back in the office. With access to Robin's calendar, location information, and a connection to the Salesforce automation software, a social platform can be aware of who Robin is talking to and then offer resources that she can use to increase the likelihood of a sale. For instance, if Robin is selling a billing system to a health insurer, the system might suggest that she "reach out to Jim, he has experience in setting up billing software for health benefits organizations," or "read this blog if you want to know more about healthcare reimbursements."

BIG DATA AND SOCIAL ANALYTICS

If you look at all the documents a person in one company writes, all the people s/he is connected to, all the interactions s/he has, things s/he "likes" or recommend and multiply that by the 500 people working at a small company, it is a lot of data. It's no wonder the amount of global digital information that the world created and shared—everything from documents to photos to status updates—grew nine times over five years.[5] By 2020, the total data generated worldwide is projected to reach over 3 million petabytes (1 petabyte = 1 million gigabytes).[6]

Social and big data are intertwined because social platforms, hosted in the cloud, use all this data to connect people to other people, topics, and documents. Some aspects of social technology could exist without big data—you could have activity streams, transparency, and groups of individuals who are interested in a specific topic—but connecting people to information and other people based on behavior depends on big data. Social at scale depends on big data to get the right information to the right person at the right time, in context. A social platform analyzes the data that traverse the platform and makes recommendations: connections that users should make, groups that specific users should join, and documents people should read.

Big data analysis can be compared to finding the needle in the haystack. Conducting this analysis and matching on a single box is impossible; one box just can't hold all of these data. When data are located in many different systems in the cloud, analysis requires processing information from many different systems simultaneously. Hadoop and other big data tools enable us to understand and make sense of connections between people and data both efficiently and affordably. Hadoop stores all the users' "likes," documents, and connections and learns what is important to each user. Then it periodically offers recommendations as to what a person should view, who they should connect with, etc.

Xerox

At Xerox, hiring for its call centers used to involve interviewing applicants and heavily favoring applicants who had previously worked in customer service. Now, Xerox leaves hiring to an algorithm. In the past, personality tests were just one tool in evaluating potential hires. Tests and data analysis are superseding interviews in importance. For Xerox, key variables for successful call center employees are the applicant's proximity to work, access to reliable transportation, and activity on one or more social networks—but not more than four. With the aid of powerful computers and sophisticated software, companies can analyze multitudes of data to both screen and predict successful applicants.[7]

Social analytics and the science of relationships provide new ways to process and mine large-scale, heterogeneous data, all of which are streaming at the speed of the Internet. As David Gutelius, chief social scientist at Jive Software suggests, social analytics are about using new techniques to cut through the irrelevant noise in the enterprise to get work done. The future of work is personalized. It's about giving people access to the right information and the right people at the right time and helping people weave their own new connections.[8]

The Social Graph

Drawing connections between users based on the user information they provide—for instance, Sally Anderson worked at Wells Fargo, so she likely knows Jeff Williams who also worked at Wells Fargo—is not a new idea. These connections rely on user self-identification. A social graph, in contrast, is the representation of relationships between people and their ideas, usage patterns, and communication. The enterprise social graph is the total social context for what businesses do. It is the organic, emergent architecture that is constantly reinventing itself as new people interact and add to it. What today's technology, specifically the social graph and artificial intelligence, can do is move a step beyond these explicit identification markers and map how people actually behave. Figure 2.1 is a representation of the social graph, showing connections between people, ideas, and content.

The biggest opportunities for the enterprise come from merging big data with the enterprise social graph. A social graph might connect two people who worked on a document together. The social graph highlights the artifact that individuals and teams created and the identities of these creators; the information that users sourced, accepted, and rejected; and, ultimately, how they solved a problem. Using the social graph, we can learn infinitely more about how people and their ideas and behavior connect than simply accepting how people self-report.

We are familiar with how this happens in the consumer world. Google launched a multibillion-dollar business by serving up search results based on the number of links associated with each bit of requested information. Google leveraged the social graph to help

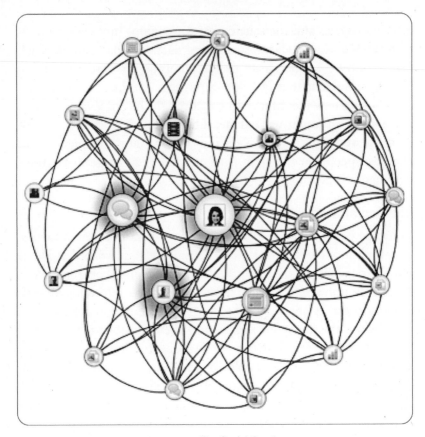

FIGURE 2.1. The Social Graph

users locate information. Similarly, Amazon suggests books, movies, or even clothing based on previous purchases and the purchases of other buyers who bought the same or similar merchandise. LinkedIn helps you grow your network by suggesting people you might know or want to know and helping you make those connections.

Facebook has become rich by collecting user data so advertisers can target consumers more effectively. Users can list marital status, age, education, and professional information as well as interests. Beyond the information that users offer, Facebook's social graph includes the connections that users form with one another, what they say, what postings they click on while using the site, and external sites they visit for news sources. The better Facebook becomes at gathering information on users and tailoring content—specifically advertisements—to users' explicit identity and behavior, the more powerful it becomes. For instance, Facebook examines a user's social graph and starts delivering advertisements for engagement rings after a user tags several pictures of herself and only one other male, she receives congratulatory postings on her wall from friends, or she posts about a planned wedding. All this happens without the woman changing her status to "engaged."

But compared to the artificial intelligence in the consumer space, artificial intelligence in the enterprise is more complex and powerful. Enterprise learning does not focus on single transactions—e.g., a user clicked on "x" so we will deliver "y" in the user's advertising display pane. Instead, enterprise social systems develop artificial intelligence by monitoring human interactions. The quality of artifacts from interactions, the complex web of team behavior, as well as social context all contribute to this artificial intelligence.

When artificial intelligence is applied in a social network, the machine figures out which individuals best fit with which information regardless of self-identification. Individuals might have deep knowledge of a certain area even if that area is outside their designated job. To leverage this knowledge, artificial intelligence develops a model of targets (individuals) by looking at everything they are saying, accessing profile information, accounting for connections with other users, recording digital gestures, etc., and creating an index. Then, when a new message comes through, the machine asks itself, "Of all the targets I have in my index, which ones best match this thing?" This information could be delivered in search results or a list of possible targets.[9] By paying attention to what people are doing in a larger complex—not what they say they do—the social platform can make suggestions and matches between users and between users and content.

The Social Graph at Work

Using the social graph and additional data sources, both internal and external to the company, a social software system can use the same techniques that Netflix uses to recommend movies to funnel the most important data to the employee who is in the best position to take action on them. The old equation is stood on its head by social platforms: Instead of you always looking for information, information is always looking for you.

When this matching between individuals and content and the social graph takes hold, the individuals we expect to be solving specific problems aren't always the ones who do. We can see how individuals come together and contribute information around a particular need. This forces down the walls between employees, partners, and consumers. In their place, new connections—and, by extension, communities—form in and between different stakeholders.

Because social business software is built on understanding a host of inputs—not just forum or blogs—it's also possible to know what a community should pay attention to before any one person on the platform mentions it. For instance, a topic like a fast-moving competitor can come up in various discussions. The social platform can route that content to those people who are in the best position to address it. This can occur even if that competitor is never mentioned in a formal meeting or included in a document.

Social business software can create bonds where they may not have existed (or may have existed in a weaker form) and make a big company work more effectively. Through monitoring what individuals say and do on the platform, the platform's artificial intelligence can highlight opportunities for cooperative innovation between product designers and sales, or collaborative problem solving between partners.

THE UNIQUE ASPECTS OF SOCIAL TECHNOLOGY

Social can seem like yet another distraction. People often dismiss the value of social in the enterprise because the way social is used in the consumer space can seem trivial and even ridiculous: "Had a great sandwich today!" "George checked in at Madison Square Garden," etc. Regardless of a person's interest in Foursquare or Facebook, however, social technology is unique and has several characteristics that distinguish it from any other communication technology we have ever seen.

Since the beginning of time, work has been social. Companies are social institutions because they consist of people. And people need to communicate. Many of the U.S.'s earliest businesses were general stores with prominent locations on a small town's Main Street. The owner of that general store was in constant communication with his or her employees on the shop floor. If he wanted to give instructions to the stock boy or coworkers, he didn't tack instructions on the wall. Instead, he tapped an employee on the shoulder and spoke to him. When the shop owner chatted with townspeople in the store, he found out which new products customers wanted and heard complaints or compliments. Communication was direct, simple, and ongoing.

Now that users are connected to one another all the time, we are more dependent on each other. We work in teams and across geographies. This radically increases the need for group productivity and social software. Not surprisingly, improvements to personal productivity—like a new version of Microsoft Office—have little impact on an enterprise's overall productivity because they don't impact how we work with each other.[10]

One of Facebook's biggest insights—now part of the definition of social—is that users have a need for passive versus active sharing. When people sent e-mails or shared photos over e-mail, it was understood that the recipient would open and reply to the message. This put a burden on the recipient. Facebook's engineers, who built technologies like News Feed, realized that giving people an option to share in a way that doesn't require a response is appealing to most people. Facebook allows users to "throw stuff out there" and other users to decide whether or not they want to view or respond to the information.

Social communication, similarly, lowers the bar for communication in the enterprise by making it acceptable to share information in less formal ways. Enterprise news feeds, for instance, are a simple and efficient way for people to share information in a company. They also encourage people within organizations to share information more readily. Company-wide memos require a lot of work and must be perfect; because the bar is high, most organizations don't produce many of them. When people post something on a social news feed, however, they understand that not everyone in the enterprise will read it and that viewers don't expect postings to be highly detailed or perfectly composed. Differing expectations for this kind of communication means that people are more likely to share information frequently.[11]

Key Differentiators of Social Technology

Centrality of Content

Social emphasizes content over content creators. Instead of content residing with individuals, data are centralized and users come to the data. In order to ensure that only those people who should see the content are able to, a content owner or community manager can change access controls that determine who is authorized to view the information. Further, issues around version control subside as the most updated copy of a document is always accessible in the cloud rather than sitting in an e-mail box, on a server, or available via a link.

Centrality of content makes for more efficient contact sharing, as Anna-Christina Douglas, head of product marketing manager at Dropbox, suggests:

> If all of your work is in one place, it's much easier to share it fluidly. Instead of e-mailing files back and forth, you should be able to go to one central location and access the most up-to-date versions. The less time people need to spend looking for their information and figuring out how to get it in the hands of the right people, the more efficient and satisfying work becomes.[12]

Activity Streams

Every social product—Twitter, Facebook, Yammer, Spigit—has its own type of activity streams. An activity stream provides, in one location, updates on people, places, projects, and content in a social network in the form of a running list. The activity stream reinforces the idea of content at the center of a network.

An intelligent social network can personalize what a person sees in his or her activity stream. Users not only see the topics and people they've subscribed to, but also see content in terms of priority.

Contextual Recommendations

Social technology makes the basic but time-consuming task of searching for information easier because it leverages patterns and connections between people and content. The software figures out which individuals best fit with which information, regardless of how the searcher or sources of information self-identify. First, it develops a model of targets (individuals) by looking at everything that people on the system are saying, accessing profile information, and accounting for connections with other users. Then, when a new message comes through, the machine asks itself, "Of all of the targets I have in my index, which ones best match this thing?"[13]

Consider two people in a software company who are looking for "analyst reports." One is a finance manager while the other is a product manager. The system knows that even though they both use the term, "analyst reports," it means something different to each: the finance manager is looking for Wall Street investment reports, while the product manager is looking for analyst reports from industry research firms like Gartner and IDC. Without asking any clarifying questions, the software delivers the right content to each individual.

Transparency

Social platforms are the antithesis of individuals working on their own computers independently. When connected to a social platform, people have the ability to work "out loud," meaning they can make all or any of their actions, comments, or gestures visible to anyone in the system. One of the several benefits of this environment is better information sharing. People can ask a question without knowing who might have the answer. This increases the chance that individuals find the information they want and that they connect with people who are likely to be able to answer related questions.

Transparency helps employees feel informed and can also drive better results for individuals as well as the firm in general. As Jordan Cohen, an expert in knowledge worker productivity, suggests, transparency can help us see all the inputs that come together in a project—market segmentation analyses, decision making in cross-functional teams, and competitive analysis. "A system that makes all these inputs visible to management," Cohen explains, "will enable better decisions." He continues:

> At a collective level, knowledge work is often interconnected: one knowledge worker's output is another knowledge worker's input, so transparency benefits the process of knowledge work as a whole. If knowledge workers and their managers can "see" the work, they are more likely to contribute additional value beyond the narrow task that they are assigned.[14]

Following, "Friending," and Connecting

Social technology enables you to connect both with people that you know offline and also individuals you don't—and might never—know. Tools like @mentioning enable these connections by ensuring that the person mentioned sees a comment, document, update, or reply. Users can subscribe to or "follow" different topics and individuals that interest them and/or are important to their jobs. Once a person is connected to a certain topic or person, s/he receives content related to the topic automatically in his or her activity stream. No more spamming an entire company with mildly relevant e-mails!

Consider a common retail industry issue: inventory control. If the inventory of a certain soccer cleat is running low at Adidas, specific people in the purchasing and retail verticals need to know this information. However, the entire company—or even all of retail and purchasing—does not. By posting in an activity stream and @mentioning specific groups, the company can be assured that the right people receive this information.

Social Sentiment Signals

Social also gives individuals the opportunity to share sentiments about a certain topic, person, or decision. With sentiment signals such as "liking," "thumbs up," or choosing to "star" a certain post, viewers give feedback in a simple and quick way. Before these social technologies, the only way people could respond after viewing content was to leave a comment.

The collected signals that a person offers and receives contribute to that individual's profile. These signals play an important role in matching people with people and people with content; what a person does supersedes what he or she says.

We've described big data, mobile, cloud, and social separately. Social technologies don't require all of these technologies—an enterprise software package like SharePoint could have an activity feed. A robust social business platform, however, sits at the intersection of all these technologies. In fact, it can't work without big data, mobile, and cloud together. In the following chapter, we'll describe how social business software takes advantage of all these technologies to enable new capabilities in the enterprise.

Exploring Social Search

Adding social context to search results gives us a wider and deeper understanding of a search. This is a complicated process as gathering context takes resources, namely the ability to analyze big data. It requires assembling heterogeneous information streams like Twitter, e-mail, Facebook, and any other data from users' searches or information sharing. Each stream leaves behind a different signature that is more complex than what the end user sees. The task of artificial intelligences is to extract something from each information stream and human activity and assemble them into a set of behaviors and actions that can inform a system, individuals, or groups.

With a targeted list and queries, the system is doing two things: matching and personalization. The system first matches a question or request for information to a target who might be able to answer to that question. Then, it personalizes or tweaks the match to each user by first understanding the person looking at a screen and a myriad of different users. Individual users might get slightly different lists of people (who could answer their question), based on who they are connected to, topical information about them, etc. The machine may also shift the rank and composition of the targets in order to give a good set of candidates to address the question.

Next, the human interaction comes in. The machine makes weak hypotheses and tests those broadly with users. By paying attention to user feedback—human interaction—the machine refines the information it has. The machine also incents targets to participate.

Sometimes these hypotheses are ignored. Other times, the system suggests a positive match and the user invites the suggested person to the forum. The machine watches what happens, records the human reactions to the information that the system delivers, and constantly learns. All of this gets built into machine learning.

It is also possible to engineer the interface to say that a person is not a good match and allow the machine to learn how users respond to this information.

Understanding Adaptive Social Computing

Social business software endowed with artificial intelligence runs little experiments over and over that tell us about nodes in the system. The software keeps track of which questions are being asked, who interacts with which features (recommendation, search), and describes the people in the system. Adaptive social computing may take different forms, but it has three key steps.

Awareness

The software is aware of context, what's happening in terms of high dimensional social activity, and why it matters in the enterprise space. In the consumer space, these activities are driving consumption. The goals of these systems are relatively simple—action, click, time on site. In the enterprise, the goal is more complex: get the right people working on the right things at the right time and solve problems. Awareness tries to take in high dimensionality, all signals and digital gestures from all systems, and track these gestures over time.

Action

The system takes its understanding of state—of you as a worker and other things in your system—and uses its power to match information to people as well as people to people. It may use automated message routing, contextual recommendations, or user-facing features.

Adaptivity

The system pushes out messages and hypotheses for users, to which users can react. The system then analyzes the signals that come out of these interactions and uses that information to update all the models in that system. This process can personalize the user experience, enable the system to swarm resources at the right time, and organize people in a new way.

The system's ability to adapt to new information also enables cognitive prosthetics (intelligence aids). It isn't just filtering the information out there but also finding the information that is just outside the user's view and bringing it into view.

If a team can complete all of these steps at any level, it can create higher-quality artifacts over time and, in turn, higher-quality results.

CHAPTER 3

NEW CAPABILITIES AND REMOVED CONSTRAINTS

SOCIAL ENABLES CREATIVITY

Social is not about breaking processes—but about capturing creativity.

—**Bill Lanfri,** early employee of SynOptics and computer networking pioneer

Why creativity? Because social technology removes constraints and inefficiencies between members of a network. It effortlessly brings together individuals who are physically separated. Because people are no longer bogged down in the complications of getting their ideas across to the right people, their creativity can flow unimpeded.

Social Is No Longer Optional

Requiring only passive participation while offering context and routing, social technology expands the capabilities and potential of teams and individuals. And instead of just managing processes and keeping a business running, enterprises can exploit social technologies to do new things. Social is no longer a "nice to have" technology. Marc Andreessen, cofounder of Netscape and LoudCloud and now a technology investor, believes social technologies are becoming a necessity for enterprises:

> Every manager knows that the greatest asset of any company
> is its people, and every manager also knows that the true
> productive potential of its people has never been fully realized.
> The opportunity with social software in the enterprise is to
> arm every employee with the knowledge, connectivity, and
> tools needed to have the biggest possible positive impact on the
> business. This is key to competitiveness—it's not going to be
> optional.[1]

Chubb: Using Social Technology to Speed Innovation and Knowledge Sharing

Innovation is one possible business outcome that arises when organizations embrace social technology. In the case of Chubb, a Fortune 500 property and casualty insurer in with $13 billion in annual revenue, 10,000 employees, and offices in over 30 countries, social technology is the key to competitiveness. Social business software enables Chubb to increase the speed of knowledge transfer, manage the pace of change, and support innovation. These are activities that Chubb could not do with any of their other existing technologies. As Jon Bidwell, chief innovation officer, explains:

> We've automated policy issuance, claims processing, and check
> issuance. We've done all we can to wring as much efficiency out
> of the organization as we can. But we really haven't been able
> to improve velocity of knowledge management, the ability to
> get information into people's hands very quickly, the ability to
> network with your peer group, to capture what people know,
> and capture experiences as they happen with our customers and
> agents and brokers. That is the business value that we're seeing
> today with social intranet. We're able to go out and solve specific
> problems very, very quickly.[2]

Beyond working faster and smarter, explains Gerry Myers, vice president of global innovation, social business software accelerates innovation throughout the company. At Chubb, social business software has created an environment where people can find each other and be "always on" for dynamic innovation, regardless of rank:

> Employees don't have to wait for an "innovation event" to pass through their branch or organization to contribute their insight and ideas. As a result, we've been able to reach down to low levels of organization—even call centers—and bring a broader range of employees into the conversation. From our experience, here innovation happens best when we find a way to generate ideas from the people who interact with our brokers and customers on a regular basis. If you can get those people empowered, you can really spur innovation.

THE INTERSECTION OF SOCIAL, MOBILE, CLOUD, AND BIG DATA TRANSFORMS THE ENTERPRISE

Many enterprises struggle to deal with the combined power of social, mobile, cloud, and big data simultaneously. Others, though, are thriving by harnessing these technologies to improve their business. Consider Amazon, a company that utilizes all of these technologies. Customers can see what their friends are reading, get recommendations based on previous purchases, read purchased content on mobile devices, and store content in the cloud. While many enterprises are overwhelmed, companies like Amazon are able to leverage these technologies efficiently. Genentech, the biotechnology pioneer owned by Roche, is another company that has developed solutions that intersect social, mobile, cloud, and big data.

Genentech

According to Andy Wang, Genentech's principal systems architect, the company is constantly looking to understand trends in social, consumer, and mobile technologies. The IT organization's

guiding strategy is IT service anytime, anywhere, to anyone using any device. Genentech has been on the forefront of
consumerization of IT—the trend of consumer technologies
migrating to enterprise computing environments. When Apple
released its first iPhone in 2007, Genentech supported over
8,000 BlackBerrys. The company realized the iPhone could radically change employee communication, immediately kicked off
an iPhone pilot, and the next day released its first iPhone app,
"Get a Room." "Get a Room" is a simple conference room sched-
uler where users can specify number of people, location, and
audio and visual requirements. It interfaces with Google calendar and comes back with possible rooms. Once the room is
secured, the app issues a receipt for the room and books time in
the calendar.

As mobile technologies have improved, Genentech hopes to
offer field salespeople iPads only—no phones, no laptops.

Improving Sales Productivity
In 2008, Genentech introduced Salesforce.com. While Salesforce
.com helped organize customer data, keeping information up-
to-date was a challenge when reps had limited time with physicians. Genentech salespeople needed to navigate several fields
and screens in the process of providing information to physicians
(e.g., checking status of reimbursement or logging interactions).
To solve this problem, IT created an app called "On the Road"
to enable the field sales team to easily interface with Saleforce
.com. When reps use On the Road to retrieve or enter information, they spend less time doing data entry and, in turn, spend
more time with physicians.

Similarly, Genentech used mobile technology to address
information management and regulatory challenges. Field salespeople wanted to establish relationships with physicians but,
legally, they couldn't discuss certain topics. For instance, only a
specific team within the company was allowed to answer questions about pharmaceuticals' off-label use. To give salespeople
an option beyond telling the physician, "I will get back to you
with the information," Genentech wrote an iPhone app called

"Get an Expert." Now, when a field salesperson meets with a physician and the physician asks a question about off-label use, the salesperson launches "Get an Expert," chooses a specific drug, and uses Skype to see who is online and who is available. When the user selects a suitable expert, "Get an Expert" initiates a Skype video call and the physician immediately connects with the expert.

Using Social Business Software to Drive Experimentation and Improve Collaboration

Social technology has enabled Genentech to become more efficient by supporting one of Genentech's driving corporate philosophies, "fail fast and fail cheap." Since implementing social business software in 2007, Genentech has encouraged groups within the organization to experiment with the software.

Consider the company's clinical development organization, a group made up of clinical operations, biometrics, and other teams. Clinical development's private social business platform, PDLive, taps into the company's repository for all clinical data and serves as a social layer on top of what many consider the firm's most impersonal information, clinical data. This group uses the platform to crowdsource suggestions for how to improve the process of running clinical trials, by far the most expensive part of the drug development process. For instance, if Genentech finds that the dosage is wrong in a particular trial, its clinicians can share this information with their peers right away on the platform and stop other clinicians from making the same mistake.

The development group uses PDLive to connect 5,000-plus product development users worldwide. It gives them a way to share their valuable intellectual property information in a secure environment. This helps reduce redundancy and prevents clinical development team members from duplicating efforts and making the same mistakes over and over.

Rather than shying away from integrating new technologies, Genentech embraces tools to both improve efficiency and work together in ways that were never possible without cloud, mobile, big data, and social tools. Social technology allows Genentech to get visibility about what people are saying, pinpoint bottlenecks, and identify key influencers to get everyone at the company the information they need to make sound decisions and, ultimately, help the patients.[3]

NEW CAPABILITIES WITH SOCIAL TECHNOLOGIES

Social software brings new capabilities to the enterprise; social business platforms take a quantum leap in simplifying information exchange. Users can have more open, natural conversations even with people they have never met. They gain the ability to recreate the kinds of conversations that were only possible when people worked alongside each other and communicated face-to-face.

But this is just the beginning.

In the social business realm, social is not about just "liking" content and "friending" other users. It's about projecting high performers' expertise and crowdsourcing new product ideas. Most importantly, though, it's about using social business software to drive business value.

Several features distinguish social technologies from other communication technologies. These attributes bring people together to make better decisions and learn more than almost any individual could on his or her own.

Figure 3.1 provides a bird's-eye view of the social technologies described in more detail during this chapter:

Co-Invention and Crowdsourcing

Before social technologies reached the enterprise, organizers used surveys or focus groups to gather feedback from large groups. They'd search for a predictive answer using the wisdom of crowds—something similar to the "ask the audience" option on *Who Wants to Be a Millionaire*. But surveys and focus groups can be both expensive and slow methods of getting the answer you want. Inviting

FIGURE 3.1. Social Technologies

many individuals to weigh in on a social network is a more efficient and accurate—and much less expensive—way of reaching the right answer or gathering innovative ideas.

Intuit

Intuit, the maker of software products for personal and business finance such as Quicken and TurboTax, wanted to leverage the knowledge within its user community to simplify financial management for users. Product managers noticed that users struggled when they answered the interview questions in the process of preparing their taxes with TurboTax. The questions seemed straightforward to Intuit, yet many users had exceptions that made it difficult to know how to answer questions. Intuit had assumed the company's numerous professional tax experts would be able to answer all user questions but, in some cases, even these experts were stumped.

The company sensed that the user base's collective intelligence could fill in where professionals could not. Intuit introduced a social module called "Live Community" to take advantage of a passionate user community and enable users to help each other. Now, when users activate "Live Community" while doing their taxes, they see a panel on the side of their screen with other users' questions, answers, and commentaries. Scott Cook, chairman of Intuit, recalled how Intuit was blown away by the results:

> Despite all of the help systems we thought were working,
> though, we were getting questions from users we never would've
> expected and never would've answered.
>
> They were reasonable questions, in fact—for example, one
> of our employees asked how to split a mortgage credit: she was
> living with her boyfriend. They had a mortgage. They weren't
> married. How do they split the mortgage so it helps both of
> their taxes? That question was not in our help systems, but it was
> asked and answered in Live Community.[4]

Expertise Location
The Rise of User-Generated Content
Social technologies make it infinitely easier for individuals to contribute comments and information on a specific topic. Once, if people needed to find a reliable source on a generally accepted answer to a question, they turned to the *Encyclopedia Britannica*. This worked if they wanted to know about dinosaurs, the Battle of Gettysburg, or Napoleon. They assumed that the *Encyclopedia Britannica* had hired people who were experts in their field and had the most accurate information.

Then came Wikipedia. Publications like Britannica that had always been the authoritative word on almost every subject questioned how Wikipedia could be a legitimate information authority. Could a self-regulating publication with user-generated content really provide accurate information? Surprisingly to many observers, Wikipedia and Britannica had similar numbers of errors. Not surprisingly, in 2012, Britannica announced that after 244 years, it would no longer publish a print edition.

In the pre-social, pre-Internet world, it was hard for ideas, movies, music, or even products to connect with their potential audiences. To gain distribution, content needed to satisfy many criteria: be from a well-known organization, follow current trends, and, perhaps most importantly, pass the culture czars' tests of what an audience would accept.

Now, not only is it easier for individuals to provide content but, as the pace of change increases, user-generated content is also becoming the only content that can keep up with the mass of information and the speed of change. The official opinion on a certain topic is giving way to individual opinions. Even our perception of the legitimacy of these individual opinions is changing. Now that it's possible to see many perspectives, we realize that what we thought were authoritative sources—encyclopedias and textbooks, among others—had their own biases.

When individuals can easily comment when information is inaccurate, collective knowledge becomes increasingly self-regulating. We took it as fact that Pluto was a planet (we now know it as a dwarf planet) or even believed that the most popular way to send messages on a mobile phone was by sending a text message. But with the world changing so quickly, only those information sources like Wikipedia that draw on collective intelligence and iterative revisions remain accurate.

Expertise Location to Drive Sales

Expertise location is also a challenge for businesses. Global sales teams—organized by region, customers, or even product lines— are often frustrated by their inability to locate team members' expertise. For instance, Ken, a sales representative in Houston, might be selling to a health insurer. Ken knows that his colleagues have sold to similar customers but can't figure out whom to ask for information about what insurance companies look for in a social platform.

Or consider Cindy, a representative in the sales department of a medical device company, MedDevice. Cindy previously worked in purchasing at a hospital. When MedDevice's New York City team has a sales opportunity at another hospital, the team tries to gathers as much information as possible on likely competitors, politics, and culture prior to a sales call. Unfortunately, only those people who work directly with Cindy or read the e-mail announcing her arrival know she previously worked at a hospital.

On a social business platform, this content is transparent. The sales team posts an update on the social business platform saying, "Looking forward to meeting the team at Memorial Hospital to talk to them about our purchasing software," and Cindy sees it. She responds, offering specific suggestions that increase the likelihood of a sale.

Expertise Projection

Every organization has at least a handful of individuals who are the "go-to" people on specific topics. When these experts have useful information, they can keep it to themselves, guess who might be interested, or send an e-mail to a large group. When they keep their expertise to themselves, they limit their reach and don't help anyone but themselves. Sharing it through e-mail to a diverse group of recipients feels like spam, at least to some of the recipients. On a social business platform, these experts can provide content whenever they like. The next time someone asks the expert the same question that s/he has already answered, the expert doesn't have to answer again. Instead, s/he enters the question in the search box and sees a list of results on a specific topic. The requestor—and everyone else in the company—has instant access to the expert's latest thinking. Once someone adds knowledge to the system, anyone can access it, forever.

Chubb

At the insurance company Chubb, the personal lines division caters to high net worth individuals and insures homes, valuable articles, collectibles, yachts, jewelry, art, etc. Scott Brown, knowledge management project manager for Chubb's personal lines division, explains that appraisers have developed valuable expertise in assessing a myriad of assets, many of which are difficult to value without significant subject matter expertise. Since appraisers are often on the road, sharing expertise with colleagues can be a challenge. On a social business platform, they can project their expertise over a wide audience, even when they are on the road:

> For our appraisers, it's feet to pavement. They're out visiting our customers and clients. With a social intranet, they are able to share their stories from those different regions and post pictures of home construction or even different types of stained glass. They might even comment on a photo of a piece of art that was damaged and explain how to restore it properly.[5]

Chubb experts don't know who will use the information they post, but they act in the certainty that it will be useful to someone, somewhere. By using the social platform, they save the next stained glass appraiser from struggling to value the asset, and experts save themselves time from having to answer each subsequent question individually.

In the case of Hurricane Irene in 2011, Chubb dealt with customers' flooded basements and other issues. Using their social platform, the appraisers were able to gather all the knowledge about managing water damage in homes following a flood. This helped them create best practices about how to talk to clients who sustained water damage in their home, and how to help prevent basement flood damage in the future. Brown was amazed by how the social business platform simplified sharing expertise:

> We've always had the intellectual capital, but to be able to harvest it, to expand upon it, and to share it and to memorialize it makes it a different, more valuable asset altogether. Now, if an agent needs to get information about a topic like "basement flood mitigation," an underwriter can simply search the social platform and up bubbles relevant content and subject matter experts, each with a picture and full profile. Subject matter experts can now comfortably crowdsource their information without making the phone calls, without going to instant messaging, or putting information in a message and never receiving a response.

When employees search for the answer to a question on a social platform, the technology takes context into account. Context ensures that the system delivers the right information to the user without the user having to clarify his/her question. For instance, when a person is on the social platform and asks a question about "framing," the system sees the other questions the individual has asked and other searches s/he has made. It knows to send information about framing heavy works of art rather than the most stable way to frame houses in earthquake zones. As Scott Brown suggests, "Social business software is becoming the big brain of our organization."

While Chubb agents push expertise to other individuals on the social platform, people who need answers can also pull knowledge from users on a social platform. A global consulting firm launched a social platform called Spark. One consultant showed she could conduct research "while she slept." A manager at the firm's office in Russia, she asked a question about tax authorities and practices in other countries. Overnight, she received 23 replies from 17 countries, effectively pulling the information she needed from many people, most of whom she did not know or didn't realize could answer her question.

Idea Sourcing

Social technologies and platforms make it easy to generate and prioritize new ideas from a wide and diverse audience.

The National Dialogue on Federal Mobility

In January 2012, the Obama White House used a social platform to initiate the National Dialogue on Federal Mobility and bring people together to develop a federal mobility strategy. The White House intended this national dialogue to direct utilization of mobile technologies to improve services to citizens, engage citizens in government, reduce costs, and increase employee productivity. By sourcing ideas through the Federal Mobility website, Steven VanRoekel, the U.S. Federal Chief Information Officer, hoped to leverage existing work, increase collaboration, and reduce duplication of efforts. VanRoekel's National Dialogue ran for just over two weeks and received hundreds of votes and ideas. One of the most valuable inputs was the suggestion to develop a government-wide shared services catalog to store code, application programming interfaces, and web services that government agencies and the public could easily access and use.[6]

Procter & Gamble's Connect + Develop

Procter & Gamble (P&G) did not have a systematic process to find new ideas and turn raw concepts into innovations. They depended mainly on developers inside the company.[7] Realizing they were missing many opportunities, P&G launched a program called Connect + Develop to spur product innovation. P&G wanted to be able to partner with small companies, multinationals, individual inventors, and even competitors. Today, P&G's Connect + Develop website is a place for inventors to submit their innovation—ready-to-go products, packaging, or commercial opportunities—for review by the Connect + Develop team. P&G also lists its innovation needs so that visitors can gauge their idea versus P&G's needs.

In 2012, P&G was looking for a technology or product that "delivers significant and long lasting repair to damaged tooth enamel and dentin." One unsolicited submission led to a joint technology agreement between Syntopix Group and P&G, and a subsequent plan for P&G to use Syntopix's topical antimicrobial expertise in its consumer healthcare brands.[8]

Collective Decision Making

Whenever individuals discuss a topic, whether live or over e-mail, they often have differing accounts of the group's decision. One simple but powerful use for social technology is to prominently note a group's final decision. For instance, prior to Black Friday, members of a retailer's marketing team take to the social platform to discuss the discount that the company will offer to shoppers who visit the company's stores on Black Friday. Participants contribute ideas, and once several people have "liked" or commented that they agree with "25 percent off all merchandise prior to 12 p.m.," the discussion monitor or group manager marks the content with a special button.

This closes the matter to further discussion. Anyone who missed the meeting or wants to check the status of the decision can easily find the group's final decision and, more importantly, the context and ideas that led to this decision.

Employee Onboarding

When new employees join an organization, they spend the first several days, if not weeks, in training and acclimating to the environment. This often includes a multiday training session. If they are savvy, they also seek out people in the organization who can answer their questions and give them the inside scoop.

A social business platform can eliminate this tedious and time-consuming process. By simply joining the social business platform, new employees can read past group discussions and get historical context around team, department, or company decisions. And, when they discover documents, they also can see context. For instance, when a new employee opens a product launch presentation, he can view discussions about what the authors wanted to include in the document and see other employees' reactions to the document.

The current training model is like standing in a desert during a flash flood; new employees get hit by tons of information, but because they lack experience, they don't have the context to make sense of it. When new employees can learn at their own pace, they can refer to discussions and expertise when they have a problem. This needs-based learning not only leads to better retention because individuals understand information in context, it also means that users don't spend time learning information that they either don't need or already know. Moreover, by using game mechanics like status and badges, participants stay engaged in training.

Address-less/Number-less Communication

E-mail will be the last generation of communication that uses numbers-based (Internet protocol) addressing. Numbers-based addressing was made for machines. Even though everyone agrees on the standards between e-mail systems, users must remember an address. Telephone, fax, and post (conventional mail) also required standard addressing systems in order to operate at scale. Today's social tools, however, don't require numbers or addresses.

On Facebook, LinkedIn, or a social business platform, the only address a user needs is a name. (When two people have the same name, the user can differentiate between them based on a photograph or additional information such as position and location.) It is possible to find people and connect even without ever browsing a company directory. When devices and people are uncoupled, individuals can remain connected to anyone they have ever met during their life. Those connections are living and breathing.

Information Dissemination

Corporate Communications

Corporate communications departments have a mandate to inform all employees of company and competitor news. But often they depend on printed magazines, electronic newsletters, and e-mail blasts. When corporate communications do support an intranet, these portals often lack visual appeal and relevant, timely information. Employees only use the intranet to check the company's holiday schedule or get information before going out on medical leave; the corporate intranet is nothing more than a repository for static company information. On a social platform, corporate communications can communicate to everyone at once at the place that is the center of their work. Further, by tagging certain content, they can ensure that those people who need to pay attention will see the content.

But it doesn't end there. Beyond just pushing out messages, the communications department can monitor activity on the platform and know who heard the message, measure their engagement level, and learn how the message reverberated throughout the company. Consider a corporate communications group that launches a new flexibility policy giving all employees the choice to work at home. After posting the policy on the social platform, the corporate communications team can view comments on this policy, understand which departments were most enthusiastic, and change the policy based on employee feedback.

Bupa

Bupa, a healthcare company with customers in over 190 countries and employees in 11 countries, wanted to transition from a service provider to a healthcare partner offering products for every stage of life. Over several years, the company had steadily acquired new ventures around the globe, increasing its footprint and range of offerings. Eventually, Bupa wanted to cross-sell its offerings, integrate acquisitions, and scale its operations, but it lacked a cohesive and unified global workforce. To do this, the company needed greater transparency and increased collaboration among employees.

Bupa's intranets provided valuable information; employees even used them on a daily basis. These platforms did little, though, to unite the company to improve processes, spur innovation, and create a strong company culture. Employees relied on e-mail, but this hampered larger conversations and broader awareness of opportunities.

Social business software helped open up communication across the company that increased employee satisfaction and engagement and feelings of connectedness. The results were measurable; when employees reported that they felt more connected, this led to higher work satisfaction. Specifically, a 2 percent increase in "connectedness" led to a 10 percent increase in satisfaction.

Apparel Retailer

Any retailer can use a mobile-enabled social intranet to disseminate information and make marketing programs more effective. While headquarters may dictate store presentations, sometimes the displays a store receives—cardboard cutouts of a celebrity endorser, for instance—don't fit in every store. Mall stores, for example, might have only a fraction of the square footage of an urban flagship. One retailer was unknowingly sending the cutouts to stores without realizing the store managers couldn't display them due to lack of space. The retailer was flushing marketing dollars down the drain.

To solve this problem, the retailer's marketing team asked store managers to take pictures of their stores and then post them on the marketing group's intranet. The marketing team quickly understood the selling environment and got a visual of what was happening in the stores without having to visit each one. The marketing group then shared these pictures with the team producing the cutouts to shorten production time. The social intranet simplified collaboration between retail partners, headquarters, and corporate marketing teams, thus saving the company time and money.

Intent/Targeted Communications

Social technologies offer the ability to communicate with the person who has the answer to your question—without even knowing that person's identity. When everyone in an enterprise is engaged on a social platform, all information requests are transparent. A user can ask a question, other people jump in to help figure it out, and the user never has to find a specific person to get the answer to that specific question.

Consider a sales rep for an accounting software vendor, Ledger. The rep is calling on a new prospect and shows the prospect a video of another customer's testimonial. Intrigued, the prospect says she wants to get connected to that customer and learn more about that customer's experience. Because the presentation and video are connected to the social platform, the rep only needs to attach a request for a customer reference to the presentation and she gets the information needed about the customer reference. The rep doesn't have to know whom to ask about the reference; automatically, the right person responds to her and gives her the customer's contact details and any other relevant information.

Contextual Communications

Users don't even have to be working directly on a social platform in order to get the benefits from it. The social platform pulls the content from the enterprise's social business platform, and brings it directly to the user. For instance, if someone is looking at a sales presentation in Microsoft PowerPoint, the user can see posts from colleagues that used the same document. This could include comments about which pages resonate best with the audience. They might also be able to see that the author of the slide deck is online and available to chat.

Ambient Awareness

A social business platform can provide value even outside the confines of an enterprise network. Many social tools enable ambient content, regardless of what applications a person is using; whatever content a person is viewing, wherever he or she is on a system, relevant information shows up on the screen.

Consider a sales representative who is working in Salesforce .com and viewing the profile for GE Finance in India, an existing customer. Without opening the social business platform, the rep sees all of the presentations that the company made to GE Finance in New York, the profile of the salesperson making the presentation, and the terms of the deal. Information from the social platform gets pulled automatically to various other applications.

Information Sharing

Instead of just bookmarking a page or sending a link, social technologies make it possible to share content in its original form. For instance, if a recruiter suggests a new team member for a workgroup, rather than sending a message with a link to LinkedIn, the recruiter clicks a button and pulls the candidate's profile directly into the discussion. The technology recognizes the data's source, in this case, LinkedIn, and the data appear just as they did in LinkedIn. Further, the information the recruiter brings to the corporate system is constantly updated to match the data on LinkedIn. This profile information can be shared with a group or even future audiences, not just those viewing the profile for the first time. This makes for fewer disruptions in work and a more seamless experience.

Embedded Experiences

Until recently, integrating data from one application to another involved multiple steps. If people were working on a written proposal, they used word processing software like Microsoft Word. If they wanted to embed a spreadsheet in a Word document, they opened Excel and copied the spreadsheet. This was time consuming, error prone, and tedious. Further, the user had to have all of the Microsoft Office applications installed to make all of these actions possible.

Embedded experiences, using the open social standard, enable seamless interaction between two cloud-based apps. If people are writing an e-mail and laying out possible meeting places for a sales kickoff, they can link in information from a travel site without going to that site and copying a link. All that the users need to do is click on certain content, enter the URL or a specific symbol, and they gain access to new applications wherever they are, without leaving the screen. This is the result of an unprecedented linking of content inside of social systems. As social systems push into the enterprise and integrate with existing systems, the social platform becomes the one interface for several applications.

Dynamic Organization

Before social networking, it was difficult—or often too much effort—for individuals to find people who shared common interests or opinions. Now Twitter, for instance, connects people who might not know each other but share an interest in a specific topic. Twitter is becoming an indispensable news source. Instead of searching the web and publications for the news and stories, Twitter enables groups of people who have topical affinity to self-assemble and share with each other information and news that they find interesting.

People can also self-organize on Twitter. Using hash tags—such as #trayvon, #occupy, #Egypt, #ArabSpring, #Libya, #Syria, and #Tunisia—users propelled mass movements. People who have innovative ideas or even extremist views no longer have to pass muster with editors in order to share their opinions. Instead, they control the platform.

Prior to the advent of these social technologies, individuals didn't have simple ways to mobilize a group of people with shared values. Today, it's easy to use a hashtag (#) to find people who have commented on a certain topic or push a message out to people who are monitoring a specific topic. This anonymous, topical-based communication is different from any broadcast or narrowcast communications of the past.

As the bestselling Brazilian novelist Paulo Coelho (*The Alchemist*) explained at Davos in 2012, "We, normal people, are empowered much more than governments. Governments, they can control a few things, but today the power finally belongs to the people."[9] Social media theorist Clay Shirky echoes this position, saying, "No one claims social media makes people angry enough to act [but] it helps angry people coordinate their actions."[10] Further, Shirky explains, "Digital networks have acted as a massive positive supply shock to the cost and spread of information, to the ease and range of public speech by citizens, and to the speed and scale of group coordination."[11]

REMOVED CONSTRAINTS

Social technologies remove constraints of time and distance. When firms are able to adjust behavior and move people from e-mail and to social technologies, they can support new capabilities like cross-functional teamwork. Distance is no longer a barrier to collaboration.

Social Expands Our Peripheral Vision

Social combines adaptive intelligence—the use of technology to enhance knowledge—to make individuals more productive. David Gutelius, Jive Software's chief social scientist, claims adaptive intelligence isn't taking work away from humans but taking certain aspects of work off the table so that humans can focus on areas where they can have the biggest impact. We spend a lot of time in search mode, either using a search engine or searching for information on our own. What we lack is a way to focus individuals' attention on the information they need to pay attention to, while filtering out extraneous information that distracts them.

We can think about our realm of work as a lane on a highway where we drive. From within our lane, we watch the cars in front of us and behind us to our left and right. We have volumes of information to process just in our own lane. But we still miss some information. What is happening in other lanes, on on-ramps, off-ramps, and alternate routes can also inform our thinking. For instance, if we hit a lot of traffic, we might consider taking an alternate route. But without accurate information as to what is happening on another road, we can't make an informed decision.

Adaptive intelligence in a social system is like helping drivers keep tabs on lane boundaries—specifically blind spots—and traffic conditions on alternate routes. It allows drivers to sense traffic and motion in large systems. Adaptive intelligence is the ability of a machine to understand the highest priority tasks and needs in a community. It is not just creating a recommendation engine but understanding the problems that members of the community are trying to solve and enabling the entire network to be more resilient and responsive.

When the noise is reduced, when individuals don't have to proactively choose to ignore specific information, dig deeper on other information, or search through reams of data for one little nugget, they are able to make decisions more quickly and those decisions are better informed.[12]

IDENTIFYING VALUE AND BUILDING A BUSINESS CASE

Enterprises may differ on how important they view particular benefits of social technology. What they share is a desire to create business value. Technology should help organizations get the information they need and make smart decisions faster. Today, however, the state of enterprise technology feels more like a box of Tinkertoys spread over the floor.

The Problem

We don't have time to assemble all the pieces that we need to make a decision. Desperate enterprise workers make strategic and operational decisions by either using the information they have available or going on a massive hunt for data. Consider, for instance, a financial services firm as it ponders adding new products in the Asian market. The first step is gathering data about other players in the market, government regulations, and the market outlook—yet it's not clear whom to ask. Who has the most experience in this market? What products have been successful? What suggestions have people working in the market, those who are closest to the customer, made?

Finding answers to these questions and making decisions today involves a lot of effort. An enterprise can consist of thousands of people, each of whom has accumulated knowledge and experiences. Still, finding the right information is hard. If you had all the information available when you needed it, you could make great decisions, but this is rarely the case.

We Struggle to Locate the Information

An organization as small as 500 people, for instance, makes major decisions in the course of doing business. It might decide when to launch a new product, whom to market to, or how to respond to competitive threats. For any of these decisions, if a person could ask the rest of the company these questions, "I'm about to do this thing, whom should I talk to about this?" "What do we know about this thing?" people could make more informed decisions. What stops people from asking these questions is not knowing the most appropriate person to ask and fear of wasting people's time. Rather than migrating beyond our immediate colleagues, we do the best we can by leveraging the network and information we have.

As a result, companies make decisions that are suboptimal. They choose which products to emphasize without access to the information they need to make good decisions. Individuals do the best job they can, make the best decisions they can make. But if they were armed with all the information that mattered, they'd have better judgment.

We Don't Have the Ability to Make Quick Decisions

The fact is, we can't rely on decision-making cycles that worked in the past. In the 1980s and 1990s, management and information systems consultants landed at a company intent on changing the strategy, reengineering processes, or both.

It could take six months to understand what was happening, three months to pitch a project that would solve the company's problems, and then a year and a half to implement their recommendations.

Similarly, during the Cold War, both the players—Washington and Moscow—and weapons were stable. Despite the inherent catastrophic capabilities of nuclear weapons, historian Paul Kennedy sums up the situation: "Yes, it's true that the two sides possessed masses of nuclear weapons aimed at each other's biggest cities, but the reality is that they were constrained by a mutual balance of terror." Each side built up caches of missiles but actually maintained equilibrium.

Whether in war or in business, long horizons for decision making weren't a problem in the past. The world just didn't change that quickly. An environment where the pace of change is constantly accelerating, however, forces everyone to be more agile. Our enemies have access to chemical weapons, can blow up a commercial airliner, and attack peacekeeping forces. We can be at war with a small group or a network of small teams. These enemies might be harder to find, but the damage they can do is unprecedented. We need to be able to take the pulse of opportunities and threats and quickly respond to them. Yet until recently we did not have the tools to disseminate and understand information quickly and then act on that information.

One of the country's most iconic food brands, Oreo, understands the power of agility. When the lights went out during the 2013 Super Bowl, Oreo captured the spotlight by tweeting, "You can still dunk in the dark." Oreo's marketing team was organized to respond quickly to a changing environment. Their move is a testament to the fact that organizations need fewer world-changing insights—for instance, retail sales are moving from brick and mortar retailers to online stores—but more "micro insights," such as the observation that Boston Marathon participants are using Pedialyte rather than Gatorade to combat dehydration. After making this micro insight, Pedialyte's marketing team could send digital coupons to these individuals and quickly get a positive return on this effort. Micro insights help businesses keep pace with the evolving environment and support continuous decision making.

Exploiting Existing Resources

Social tools help organizations do more with what they already have. Particularly, social tools enable a company to get more value from its existing employees, particularly interaction workers. Interaction workers are those employees who solve complex problems that require independent judgment but also access to information and external collaboration. They are the engine of many modern firms and the fastest-growing category of workers in advanced economies. They aren't frontline employees like cashiers or clerks, nor are they production workers like construction and factory employees. Interaction workers are the professionals—the managers and consultative salespeople. They require more education and training than both transaction and production workers, and earn higher compensation than workers in either of these two groups. These workers are approximately 44 percent of a firm's workforce yet represent 60 percent of the cost.[13]

Most enterprises reflect a normal distribution; the majority of workers are average performers, while at the tails lie both underperformers and high performers. Can you increase productivity by replacing all average and underperforming workers with high performers? Nice idea, but it's neither feasible nor affordable for any company. However, unlocking these individuals' potential is far cheaper and easier than acquiring super-special talent. You can use what you have instead of continually searching for new products or human resources.

Social business software helps organizations make the best decisions possible at every juncture. A company selling data storage might have a sales team that includes specialized functions for pricing and developing RFPs. But once everyone across the sales team becomes more knowledgeable, the need for these specialized teams goes away. Armed with access to the right information, every person in the sales organization can fill out a statement of work on his or her own.

Accelerating Through the OODA Loop

Social technologies and artificial intelligence are enabling companies that truly do "know what they know." When an enterprise knows what it knows, it's able to be dynamic, agile, and responsive. Employees can make informed decisions without spending too much time searching for information.

First, consider the evolution of decision making in the military. USAF Colonel John Boyd, a Korean War fighter pilot, discovered that in dogfights, regardless of technological superiority, the United States was losing. Most people believed the plane and its technology were the key competitive advantage. Boyd concluded that it wasn't the technology that people were using that improved performance; it was the time it took them to go through the decision loop of OODA, or "observe, orient, decide, and react," a combat strategy that he developed. The enemy pilots had the ability to go through the OODA loop faster than the American pilots.

Boyd developed the "Aerial Attack Study" to codify air combat. While most pilots dismissed the idea of air combat as a science, Boyd believed that for every maneuver, there was a series of counter-maneuvers, and a counter for every counter. His flying code explained the options available to each pilot when responding to adversaries. Once the United States started to retrain pilots on the decision loop, their performance improved. This study changed the way every air force in the world fights and flies.[14]

Similarly, Citi can proceed through the OODA loop to accelerate decision making. For instance, Citi finds out that Bank of America has a hot new mortgage product. The press responds and other industry players begin to react. This is the OODA loop:

Observe: The first step is to observe the situation. A social business platform can collect all the intelligence from internal and external sources—internal discussions, Twitter, LinkedIn, banking trade rags, etc.

Orient: Once the product managers at Citibank have sense of the terrain, they must orient themselves into a position where they can make a decision. A social business platform can bring the internal team together in one place to look at all relevant information.

Decide: The social business platform helps users take the analysis they've done and the product of that analysis and put it into a virtual war room. The senior decision makers come together to make a decision.

Act: The ultimate step of carrying it out. Once you act, you want to observe how you have done. Citi launches a competing but superior mortgage product, and all product managers and branch managers discuss the results on the social platform.

Accelerating through the OODA loop isn't a new idea. What's new is the advent of technology, particularly social, to enable companies and individuals to proceed through the loop more quickly.

SOCIAL BUSINESS IMPLEMENTATIONS: THREE APPROACHES

Social business software evangelists talk a lot about connecting an entire company. In the interim before everyone is on the platform, there are three value approaches that companies can take to create value with social software, as shown in Figure 3.2. These approaches are aspirational, enterprise-wide implementations; functional/departmental rollouts; and pain-relief projects.

McKinsey & Company and Oxford University showed that one in six IT change initiatives overruns its budget by 200 percent and takes about 70 percent longer to implement than originally planned.[15] Given this failure rate, we suggest a company start an initial engagement wherever the team can demonstrate business value very quickly.

Starting with a specific group in a company that can quickly demonstrate value is a lower risk and faster way to initiate social business software in an organization than embarking on an organization-wide rollout. A specific group can build momentum and develop a cadre of enthusiastic users. The first users should be able to demonstrate a positive impact from using the

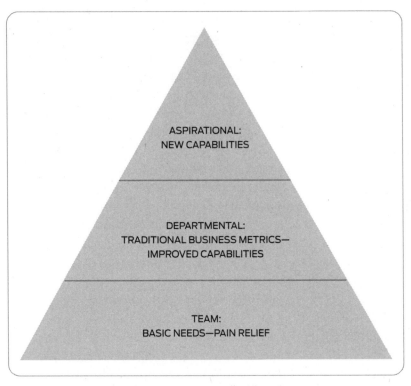

FIGURE 3.2. Implementation Hierarchy

product and have a specific need and a business problem they are trying to solve. This method also enables a company to take a lean approach to an implementation. The company focuses on just one user group at a time, solves their problems, and then continuously improves the platform before rolling it out to the entire firm. The company can take risks and fail without the ire of millions—or billions—of users.

Aspirational, Enterprise-wide Implementations

Some visionaries are so excited about the potential of social software in the enterprise that they roll it out to their entire company right away. They are the early adopters. Their vision of the future is a transparent, networked workplace. They feel that the sooner they adopt a social solution for an entire business, the faster the business will become a connected enterprise.

The aspirational level of social business software—the state where all the information you need gets pulled to you in the simplest and easiest way possible—is at the top of the social business hierarchy. Think about Maslow's hierarchy of needs. Basic needs—food, water, and sleep—are at the bottom, success is higher up, and at the apex are transformation and self-actualization. In the social business hierarchy, we see a similar progression.

Aspirational projects, also known as wall-to-wall social business platform implementations, are the cases that industry analysts and vendors have been espousing for the past five years as the be-all and end-all for enterprise social. When everyone in an organization is using the social platform, it's easy to locate expertise, content, conversations, and get all enterprise knowledge in one place. Firms develop new capabilities to do things that are only possible when the entire company is connected.

While enterprise solutions are important, they are overemphasized and aren't the best choice for the first social implementation in a firm. First, the grand value propositions that these implementations promise require a large, heterogeneous group to change. Second, an enterprise rollout often means going from no one using the software to everyone engaged on the platform. Anyone who's worked in a large organization knows this is a challenging proposition. Success requires executive leadership, yet these people have limited time. Some companies manage to get a large, distributed organization engaged on a social platform, but many get stuck with IT-led projects that never move past a pilot.

Pain-Relief Projects

At the lowest level of the pyramid are the social business software implementations for pain relief. These are the instances where small groups need a tool just to function. These groups are often similar across companies and industries. They have high swap in/swap out of employees, physical separation of workers, and visibility to communication and the enterprise as a whole. After a workgroup implements social, people in other parts of the business who are touched by that workgroup often adopt the technology as well.

Direct Business Value Rollouts

Workgroup pain-relief projects and enterprise aspirational projects sit at opposite ends of a spectrum. In the middle are the projects where social business software drives direct business value. It's about helping the business function better today by using social technology to support deal management, accelerate sales onboarding, improve customer service, and manage marketing programs, among other activities.

Enterprises that implement social business software at this level strive to improve the metrics by which they and others—investors, partners, and customers—judge them. They have a department or business function that they are trying to improve, and by using social software, they change out the "old way" of doing a specific operation for the new, social way. When a company focuses on a specific business function or activity, social business software enables it to raise the top line by increasing revenue, increase the bottom line by lowering costs—or both at the same time.

Though enterprise-wide social implementations get the most attention, that crucial space between "no one is on it" (the absence of use) and "everyone is on it" (company-wide adoption) is the best place to start. If you roll out the platform to everyone at once, it's very difficult to teach so many people how to do their jobs on a new platform; they either don't use it or use it only for simple communication.

It's also easier to demonstrate value to a decision maker when you start with a functional team or department. You can show hard dollar savings, returned productivity, and speed to outcomes or improved outcomes when you have some practical results. These results ultimately translate into business objectives like customer satisfaction, reduced operational costs, or improved revenues. Further, these functional projects take less executive commitment. When a social business solution targets a functional group, the leader can be a department or business function manager.

SOCIAL BUSINESS SOFTWARE
FOLLOWS NETWORKING'S EVOLUTION

The Evolution of Networking

High-speed computer networking actually began in enterprises in the mid-1980s as a workgroup solution; only later did it become an obvious enterprise-wide application. One type of workgroup arose around specific applications (e.g., oil exploration, aircraft design, or high-speed securities trading). These groups required high-speed networking to connect the group's powerful new workstations. IT departments in these organizations set up small, purpose-specific networks for these workgroups. The networks were very hard to change and isolated from the rest of the company. Yet, they delivered great value to the workgroups that used them and, as a result, to the organization as a whole.

The other workgroup networks that formed during this period were more informal; they sprang up following the rapid increase of unconnected PCs in the workplace. Early adopters often bypassed IT completely and bought networking equipment from computer stores; they did whatever it took to get their jobs done. Often, they would snake cables between their cubicles and connect the PCs to a file server under a team member's desk. They wanted to enable sharing of high-speed printers and larger files and replace the old "sneakernet" (saving files on floppy disks and then walking them around from PC to PC).

As these informal workgroups grew, their reliability and the growing amount of critical corporate data trapped on unreliable (and theft vulnerable) under-desk file servers emerged as serious issues. People who were already using these networks understood their value. To make these networks a robust part of the enterprise fabric, however, high-speed networks had to become enterprise grade in terms of their flexibility, security, and ability to support mission critical applications.

In the late 1980s, new technologies came to market that made it almost as easy to implement and move reliable high-speed networking connections as it was to install telephones. Subsequently, many large organizations started to deploy these enterprise grade networks. In the companies with existing early adopter workgroups, the informal wires came out from under the cubicles; the file servers came out from under the desks and into secure computer rooms; and many of the inflexible specialty networks were connected back into the rest of the company. Other organizations—those that hadn't had large numbers of isolated high-speed workgroups—simply began with enterprise implementations. Before long, company-wide deployment of high-speed computer networking became the norm.

These new networks were initially successful at process improvement, or what Lanfri called "old things done in a new way," such as sharing files and printers. As wall-to-wall networking become more commonplace, however, a new set of capabilities emerged, something Lanfri refers to as "new things done with the new way." E-mail or shared calendaring, for example, had not existed before because they only made sense once almost everyone in an enterprise was on a corporate network. Today, we take these enterprise-wide communication platforms for granted.

The Roots of Social at EMC

The first instance of a social business platform at EMC was around 2003. It was a project under someone's desk—EMC created a community and then experimented with its features

It was a "pain implementation." Teams had no way to engage with existing customers, prospects, partners, and employees and share content with them on a very immediate basis. The information they could provide often got buried in the depths of a website. EMC tried to get information to these parties through e-mail marketing or Google SEO activities or even at a live event. But giving partners and customer access to product updates and free downloads was a problem.

Though it might not have been the most productive use of a social business platform, product and sales teams found the platform made it easy to spin up a website that could act as a partner portal, support community, or hub for product launches, beta tests, labs, downloads, and videos. Essentially, the platform was a workaround for overloaded web developers and IT groups.

Any team that wanted to created a website-like presence on the web could avoid a long development process starting with wireframe designs and a list of features such as Twitter feeds and blogs. Previously, launching an online presence meant building a solution for every request.

Once one business group used the social platform, others wanted a similar solution. The product spread via grassroots adoption.

Social Business Software—a Technology Whose Time Has Come

We expect that social business adoption will follow the same enterprise adoption pattern that occurred in high-speed computer networking. In social business software, everyone can envision the big connected social company, yet this is extremely hard to accomplish with an initial implementation. Networking vendors initially faced headwinds trying to sell the big connected company; and social business software vendors will likely also experience frustration trying to convince enterprises to connect an entire company all at once. Instead, an incremental approach to what is, in essence, a new networking solution, will likely work best. First, build smaller projects, such as pain-relief implementations or enable powerful new capabilities within certain departments or functional areas. This spurs adoption across the company and is the fastest way to demonstrate value and, eventually, connect everyone in a company.

Sometimes, the need precedes the technology. In the case of organizational knowledge management, technology has finally caught up—if not surpassed—the need to arm workers with the information they need, when they need it, in context. The knowledge management system (KMS) pioneers of the 1990s had a vision of an organization where it was easy to identify valuable knowledge, share and capture best practices, promote organizational learning, and, eventually, spur innovation. But the vision was ahead of the technology needed to support it. The systems were difficult to update, only available on desktops connected to a corporate network, and lacked artificial intelligence (i.e., a person who wanted information had to know who was the best person to ask). The biggest problem was that the system was only as robust as the investment that people made in it, but the burden of maintaining the knowledge base fell on employees, many of whom were top performers.

Interestingly, when engineers built new networking hardware in the 1980s, their goal was to provide cost effective, universal high-speed connectivity. But the personal computers of that era weren't yet up to the task; they had no connectivity capabilities and insufficient computing power to function in a universally connected world. Network architects had envisioned that connected world, but the technology to truly connect everything didn't exist.

Finally, the technology for true knowledge management has caught up with the need. Like e-mail or networking in its nascent stages, social technology initially looked like a "nice to have"—but in today's world where change is happening so quickly, it has become a "must have." Companies that don't embrace social technology will lack the ability to take advantage of a rapidly accelerating pace of business.

We Have the Tools for Transformation

In Maslow's hierarchy, you need to eat before you can experience self-actualization. With a social business platform, you must be in the place where the value is very clear and, over time, grow to a wall-to-wall solution. The social business platform provides the fabric that connects everyone at the organization together to support innovation and excellence. As Lanfri suggests:

> The transformation and socialization of existing business
> processes can be a great entry point for social when there is a
> clear ROI impact versus current processes. But what I see as
> even more powerful is that a full enterprise implementation
> can enable a company to do things it has never done before and
> accelerate the pace of creativity and innovation in unimaginable
> new ways.

Working on a social business platform increases efficiency and, in many cases, revenue and profitability. While these things are important, after living through the evolution in networking, Lanfri also feels that a social business platform can ultimately enable new ways to work and create:

> While we often talk about a social network as a new thing, in a way it's really an old thing—person-to-person communication—at scale. Social business platforms give enterprises a structured way to capture and organize this critical communication at scale and extend its reach. Sure, this technology supports and improves existing business process, but more importantly, it can also encourage innovation. It captures "aha" moments, puts them into the system in a very organized way, and makes them instantly available throughout the organization. If you want to disseminate ideas with twenty-first century speed and scale, you can't use old tools or hope this will "just happen."

CHAPTER 4

BUSINESS DRIVERS AND VALUE FRAMEWORK

INTRODUCING A SOCIAL BUSINESS PLATFORM TO THE ENTERPRISE

Is Social Even an Option?

The statistics are enticing but, still, companies have questions:

> How do you bring a social platform into an enterprise setting?
> We are already struggling with ERP, CRM, business intelligence,
> virtualization, manufacturing, and human resources software.
> Where does a social business platform fit among all these?

If starting over and ripping out all existing systems were an option, you might jump at the chance to clean house. You could start with a clean slate and put everything in the cloud. It sounds enticing, but going this route would, by definition, disrupt the normal course of business.

Firms aren't always convinced a social business platform is a good investment.[1] They've been burned by expensive and tedious technology implementations. ERP systems, in particular, involved painful implementations because companies had to halt business on one system and move to a new system. Companies want an evolutionary approach to social business that leverages the IT investments they have already made. They wonder what will happen to all of their ongoing processes if they implement a social business platform. If everything is already working together, albeit not as smoothly as the company would like, how does it move to a new system without interruption?

Sometimes a social business platform replaces an inferior yet popular technology. E-mail, for instance, is entrenched in almost every company. Enterprises depend on e-mail for decision making, discussion, and processing—yet it wasn't designed for and isn't really capable of these tasks. To find a specific answer or spark discussion, a sender has to either know who has the answer or spam a large group of people. Neither of these is a great option. Without artificial intelligence, though, senders can't target an e-mail to someone they don't know but who may have the answer they need.

Marc Andreessen, technology thought leader and investor, and creator of Mosaic, the first Internet browser, says e-mail persists because of the network effect—everyone is on it. Challengers have to offer far better value than e-mail if they want to overcome the value proposition of "everyone already has e-mail."[2]

You may hold tightly to problematic technologies because they are so ingrained in your operations. If e-mails, for instance, don't get to the right recipients or get lost in a crowded inbox, people miss crucial input enabling them to do their jobs effectively and/or further a company's strategy. It's difficult to see a path toward social when no one is giving you a map. And, it isn't clear what happens when a traditional business culture intersects with the latest technology.

All of this is overwhelming. A social business platform can have a major impact on an organization; but introducing a social product and seeing if it catches on, or even asking IT to implement it are two approaches that will almost certainly fail. The two most important things you must do for a successful rollout are the following:

Focus on a specific problem you want to solve and let the business people—not IT—run the implementation.

Find the problem that, when solved, will provide the most value for your company.

When your team has a powerful new way to get the job done, work becomes more enjoyable, more cost-efficient, and produces better results. Once you have identified the problem, you can approach it with one of three proven rollout models: aspirational, business value, or pain alleviation.

THE ASPIRATIONAL IMPLEMENTATION: VALUE, PAIN POINTS, AND CASE STUDY

Connecting everyone in an enterprise creates an environment that can realize all the promises of a social business platform; a state where everyone connected to an enterprise—employees and executives and, in some cases, customers and partners too—share information effortlessly. These enterprise-wide implementations are often called "wall-to-wall," because they integrate every department and physical location in an enterprise.

When firms can gather and make sense of the information they have within their network, they can force change with new products and solutions for customers. Unlike automation technologies, social technologies don't just support "doing the same things better." Instead, they're about creating an environment and connections that enable a company to do things it couldn't attempt before. This could include getting departments to work together to make a new product, gather customer feedback and iterate a service offering on the fly, or respond to market conditions in a new way. Jeffrey Cohen, Jon Katzenbach, and Gus Vlak claim that this coordination is an art, but an essential one if a company wants to transform an interesting idea into a company-wide innovation.[3]

Now, the bad news. A successful enterprise-wide solution is the hardest kind of social business platform implementation to pull off, for the very reason that makes it most valuable: an enterprise social solution works best when everyone in the company is engaged on it. Yet achieving this networked state is not easy.

Still, the rewards of a wall-to-wall enterprise social network are massive. When employees can work and collaborate in one place, they are more productive and more capable of delivering results against the company's strategy. The platform becomes the place where work gets done in the company; it replaces e-mail, phone calls, and videoconferencing with one communication platform that connects employees, customers, and partners and integrates with the existing workflow.

Employees get the right knowledge when they need it. They can easily tap the power of the company's network. Instead of focusing on nonproductive activities, organizations can focus and align their people with the organization's strategic priorities. The results are measurable.

Driving Employee Engagement

Social platforms impact job satisfaction. According to Ray Wang, CEO and analyst at Constellation Research, engaged workers are happier and stay longer in their positions. Workers who participate in a forum, help out a colleague in a chat, or provide feedback on an enterprise initiative are 37 percent more likely to stay with their employers than employees who do not do these things.[4]

The problem is that in many distributed organizations, employees feel isolated. For instance, a person working in sales will interface with marketing and other members of the sales department. But they lack visibility into other parts of the company. They rarely see the entire sales cycle from product development to customer receipt. Work becomes increasingly compartmentalized, individuals struggle to stay on top of everything that is happening in the company, and with limited contact to people outside their operations, employees have few chances to hear about projects outside their immediate vicinity.

Considering the work environment, it's no wonder that the statistics on employee engagement are weak. According to Gallup, 71 percent of American workers are "not engaged" or "actively disengaged" in their work. This means only about a third of U.S. workers are happy to be at work and have their head in the game.

Towers Watson found that one reason that two-thirds of employees don't feel engaged at work is that "Technology continues to escalate the pace of change and alter the nature and structure of work itself, but the work environment and experience aren't keeping pace."[5] In other words, we've got cool, engaging technology everywhere we look—except at work. Work just isn't fun.

Employees' workplace engagement and a company's overall performance have a strong correlation.[6] Almost every company sees a connection between employee engagement and value. Some— Starbucks, Limited Brands, and Best Buy—can precisely identify the value of a 0.1 percent increase in engagement among employees at a particular store. At Best Buy, that increase translates into a $100,000 bump in annual revenues at that location.[7]

Employee engagement is also a leading indicator of overall corporate financial performance. Companies rated in the top 25 percent in employee engagement metrics posted earnings per share (EPS) growth nearly 9 percent higher than EPS growth of comparable companies that had lower employee engagement scores.[8]

Highly educated workers, often a large percentage of the company's knowledge workers, are the most difficult—and expensive—to replace. The accepted estimate for the cost of turnover is approximately 100 percent to 150 percent of an employee's annual salary. From this estimate, based on an employee base of 5,000 with an average salary of $45,000 per year, a mere 1 percent decrease in employee turnover could result in $1 million in annual savings. Additionally, workers between the ages of 30 and 64—extremely valuable employees at most companies—often have the lowest engagement.[9] It pays to keep employees engaged and happy in their jobs.

Aspirational Implementation: Strategic Alignment
Value Proposition
As companies grow, either through mergers and acquisitions or organically, it gets harder to connect employees to the organization's goals and to each other. Multiple time zones, distance, and the general anonymity of big companies become major hurdles. Anyone who has been in this situation understands that accessing

the information you need to make good decisions becomes a job in and of itself.

Company alignment with the strategy is a major concern for executives, yet they don't have a plan to make this alignment happen. Each employee and each unit should understand their role in implementing the company's strategy. But how do you get everyone on board with the strategy when they are physically separated and rarely interact with people outside their silo?

Social business platforms improve strategic alignment throughout the organization by mimicking the casual familiarity that you have when you interact face-to-face. If you worked in a small company with only one office, everyone would understand the company's strategy and his/her personal role in meeting company goals. When you work in a distributed firm, the social platform effectively substitutes for proximity and a small-company feel. Companies that use a social business platform for strategic alignment are able to increase employee productivity by 15 percent, reduce employee turnover by 24 percent, and, most notably, grow revenue by 3 percent.[10]

Flow[11]

To successfully develop and execute a corporate strategy, you need to do three things well. First, in addition to evaluating market opportunities and defining the company's unique strengths—all the traditional steps of developing a strategy—you have to gather input from employees.

Informal discussions, not off-site meetings, are where people make 77 percent of all strategic decisions. The company has to have a way to capture these conversations and make them available to a wider audience. When you overlook this step, employees aren't wedded to the final strategy. In fact, people who are part of creating a solution are five times more committed than people who are not.

Second, companies must make fast, informed decisions. They need to be able to quickly access facts and opinions from across the company and even from customers, partners, and experts. In many cases, gathering all these facts and opinions is one step that slows down the process. When you don't have the information to make a decision, you might miss opportunities to launch a new product or fix an existing one.

Third, the company has to change employees' behavior. The way to do this is to communicate stories about employees that are on board with the new strategy and impacting the company's success. You can do this through blogs, in-line responses, and even polls. Another method is to role model the behaviors you want. If the strategy for a gas-engine automaker is to become the top seller of hybrid cars, a manager could post information as to how the automaker's fuel economy compares to the competition's. These tasks can seem like optional actions, but without a plan for behavioral change, a business strategy will be less effective.

Pain Points

Strategic alignment—creating that feeling of one company going after a set of specific goals—is difficult without a central dynamic and flexible communications tool. Firms can't fully engage their employees when they're unable to tap into informal conversations that take place in the halls, over e-mail, on the phone, or even in meetings. It's not a matter of information gathering; companies are great at gathering information from various sources. What they struggle with is organizing and acting quickly on the information. Your firm may set a sound strategy, but company-wide e-mails and holding town hall–style meetings aren't enough to get employees aligned with the strategy.

When you use a social business platform for strategic alignment, you can access the entire workforce as a sounding board, get direct input on options, raise awareness of strategic priorities, and communicate the company's direction. Companies that have done this have seen productivity soar: 29 percent of users say they better understand their company's strategic goals, 61 percent say they are more aware of activities going on outside their immediate organization, and 26 percent say they are more able to focus their work.

When your employees can contribute to strategic decisions and see how their work aligns against strategic priorities, they are more committed and engaged—and happier. And when people stay in their jobs, you don't have to train new employees. At organizations that implement a social business platform, 61 percent of employees feel more connected to their colleagues, and 38 percent say they have higher job satisfaction. These factors contribute to revenue improvement of 3 percent.

Case Study: Alcatel Lucent[12]

After a 2011 mega-merger, Alcatel-Lucent's new management had to do what some thought was the impossible: leverage expertise across the companies, pursue global opportunities, and unite its 76,000 employees in over 130 countries. It was time to reap the synergies the company had promised investors. Considering the $21 billion telecom services and equipment company was still absorbing its 2006 acquisition of Lucent Technologies, this was an especially lofty goal. Now, it needed to also unite workers of a U.S.-based and a France-based company into one international firm.

It was difficult for employees to see outside their immediate department. They had very limited visibility to the top of the organization or across to other departments. Management also lacked visibility to other layers in the organization. They made decisions in isolation and inadvertently overlooked a lot of the best of global knowledge. Because many employees had no connection to the executive team, they focused on doing their jobs, not fulfilling the company's larger mission. As one senior executive explained:

> We have the usual challenges of a large global company and too often individuals have little visibility into what is going on beyond their own team, even in some cases when that could make a difference in the work they are doing.

Alcatel-Lucent recognized that its employees weren't satisfied and weren't bought-in to the strategy. The company realized it would have to develop a strategy alongside employees, not push one on them. The strategy had to be actionable and employees needed to support it.

Alcatel-Lucent wanted to enable employees to work across organizational and geographical boundaries. They had an intranet, but it lacked social features to facilitate group discussion and engagement. The company had multiple collaboration tools, but unless you already knew about them, it was unlikely that you would stumble on them and discover things of interest. Once the company finalized its new strategy, it planned for the social business platform to be the place where employees would learn about, build on, and commit to the new strategy.

Implementation

Alcatel-Lucent wanted a social platform that wouldn't be just another tool. It would be the place employees went to get work done. This meant it had to be accessible from anywhere, anytime, without connecting to the VPN. The company hand-selected 100 people from across the company as the first users of its social platform, Engage. The project progressed quickly; the period from contract signing to production was only three weeks. From the first 100 users, employees spread the word about Engage virally. Within three months, the company already had 10,000 users on the platform's mature version.

This rapid uptake was surprising to Alcatel-Lucent. The company had done little to publicize the tool, and the main users weren't part of the social networking generation. Jem Janik, enterprise community manager, recalled:

> We have a mature workforce so we thought it might take some effort to get them using social business tools. The fact that they joined so readily speaks to the pent-up need and the willingness of this team to experiment and try new things. Earlier file sharing platforms didn't meet this technically savvy group's expectations of speed and efficiency, but with Engage, users could sign up, launch a group, or start a discussion, and start working without any assistance. People really took advantage of that.

Results

Alcatel-Lucent used the social platform to solve a specific problem: formulate, provide feedback on, and execute the company's strategy. Executives kicked off the strategy discussion by blogging about their observations and their initial vision for the company. They then created a set of discussions around four key strategic topics and invited broad employee input. Based in part on this feedback, they determined the best strategic direction for the company and began to share it with employees on the social business platform. Employees asked about the actual plan and clarified certain points with executives and leaders.

The social business platform became integrated into the company's business. By giving all employees access to valuable company knowledge and connecting them to subject matter experts, employees can become better at what they do. Even senior management was blogging on the platform, and thousands of employees could view his posts. Janik explained that "Now employees feel they have a real dialogue with the senior leadership. It's made us more of an open culture, and it's increased broad participation and effective decision making." Here are just a couple of examples of the tool in action:

Before their annual leadership meeting, Alcatel-Lucent held company-wide discussions on Engage. They gathered concerns and feedback and used them to set the meeting's agenda. Management was able to get the pulse of what was happening in the business because, for the first time, employees' questions and answers and discussions about products and markets were transparent to the entire company.

A product group wanted to brainstorm concepts for new mobile apps, so it created a group in Engage. They'd hoped to come up with 100 ideas in two weeks, but generated 200. The low barrier for open collaboration brought many new ideas into the fold.

The platform also became an internal support tool. IT now launches all new projects on the social business platform, and whenever users encounter problems, IT and users publically document lessons learned. Each person at the company can now solve her own IT problems and wastes less time trying to manage with new technology.

As of early 2013, about 75 percent of the company's 77,000 employees had joined the community. Over 70 percent of these users agree that using the social business platform has increased their understanding of their colleagues and the business, beyond their workgroup or team. Now that people are working smarter and more efficiently, employee productivity has risen by 7.5 percent.

Identifying Product Malfunctions in Record Time

When companies, or their customers, have an issue with a product, the biggest challenge is often figuring out what's wrong. Alcatel-Lucent was fortunate to have a social business platform when one of the hardware products it supported had an antenna problem.

The problem surfaced over time. First, users from across the country entered information on the platform about problems with phone reception. Engineering monitored these isolated incidents and tried to diagnose the source of the problem—Was it regional, limited to one factory, or limited to one part? The triage and diagnosis involved several individuals in various parts of the organization.

By collaborating on the platform, the engineering team was able figure out how to fix the problem. The platform helped diagnose, solve, and communicate the solution to the organization and all customers.

BUSINESS VALUE IMPLEMENTATIONS: VALUE, PAIN POINTS, AND CASE STUDIES

While the value that a wall-to-wall implementation can deliver is tempting, especially after seeing results like Alcatel-Lucent's, the best way to eventually reach enterprise value is to start small. First introduce a social business platform as a way to create value for a specific function or business unit.

There are at least eight ways that social technologies can add value in organizational functions and span several organizational functions, including product development, operations and distribution, marketing and sales, customer service, and business support.

We're focusing on four specific instances where social business tools can enable value creation for a specific activity or function:

- ► Deal management
- ► Sales enablement

- ▶ Marketing design and execution
- ▶ Customer service

Deal Management
Value Proposition

In most organizations, members of the sales team spend a lot of their time physically out of the office. The phone is a great tool, but organizing conference calls is time consuming and tedious (and often the calls aren't very productive). When sales teams are global—organized by region, customers, or even product lines—it's hard to find the expert you need, especially using clunky company directories that are difficult to access. Even when salespeople can reach a directory from a mobile device, they see only employees' roles, titles, and responsibilities. These listings reflect nothing about a person's knowledge and connections.

A social business platform improves deal management by decreasing the time it takes to close a deal—the deal cycle time—and increasing sales per representative. Using a social business platform, companies have been able to decrease deal cycle time by 22 percent and increase the number of deals per year by 8 percent.

You shrink the deal cycle time when you get proposals (RFPs) out quickly. Using a social platform, sales teams can develop RFPs 25 percent faster. With the long process of writing the RFP out of the way, reps can focus on spending more time with customers.

Relationships drive revenue. With more direct customer contact, reps push the average deal size up by 5 percent and the team wins deals 12 percent more frequently. An added bonus is that, 57 percent of the time, the team produces a better quality pitch. Enterprises that introduce a social business platform for deal management find that revenue improves by 8 percent per rep and overall firm revenue rises by 1 to 2 percent.

Better performance, fewer frustrations, and tighter connections between employees also reduce salesperson turnover. Sales teams capture customer information that isn't in a CRM system without doing any extra work.

Flow

The deal management process is similar in most organizations, and it's rarely smooth. It typically has five main steps: lead qualification, opportunity development, the pitch, negotiation, and deal closing. Usually, an inside sales representative qualifies the lead and then turns it over to the field sales representative. The field rep prepares a pitch for the meeting and, if s/he has product-related questions, turns to the product specialist. The rep's manager coaches the rep and helps answer questions about pricing, discounting, and structuring the deal. Once the field representative completes the pitch, s/he presents it to the customer. If the customer is interested, the field representative works with the product specialist to prepare a quote. Then the field representative reviews, presents, and negotiates the quote with the customer. Sales management approves discounts and provides overall guidance. Finally, the field sales representative presents the quote to the customer.

Pain Points

The process involves many teams and, individuals and opportunities for mistakes, delays, and confusion. First, field representative aren't always consistent in the way they record customer information; some are very detailed while others are not. Secondly, field representatives, especially those who are new to the company, struggle to find the very person who can answer their question. It would be great if they could huddle product experts, sales support, and sales operations, but, instead, the rep ends up talking to each party independently.

During the process, field representatives are supposed to capture customer feedback. Some do this very well, but others ... not so much. Product specialist can't always find the most recent information they need to make an accurate quote—that is, if they even know what information they're missing. The negotiation process is a painful coordination of sales management and specialists. Finally, when the whole process ends, most reps just want to move on to the next deal and skip the tedious process of writing up customer feedback. Figures 4.1 and 4.1A illustrate the pain points that many companies face when managing deal flow.

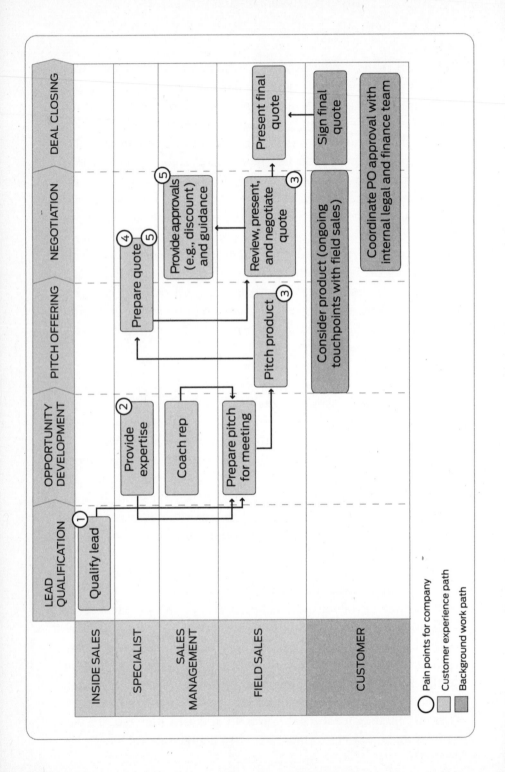

Pain points for company

Customer experience path

Background work path

1. Inconsistent capture of customer information

2. Difficulty finding and collaborating with experts, sales support/ops

3. Inconsistent capture of customer feedback

4. Failure to find the most recent information to prepare accurate quote

5. Trouble coordinating an increasing number of internal stakeholders

FIGURES 4.1 AND 4.1A. Deal Management: Common Pain Points

Case Study: Global Accounting and Consulting Firm

A global accounting and consulting firm of 182,000 employees in 148 countries wanted to make its multinational company feel small (at least to its employees). The firm was as complicated as it gets in terms of organizational structure. It had a complex organizational structure that created challenges when implementing a "single instance" social tool.

It needed to be easy to find people and bring fragmented groups together, accelerate insights, and get bids to clients faster than any other firm. The firm's work involved bidding and proposing projects to clients and then completing the consulting, advisory, audit, or tax project. Though collaboration across the firm was integral to almost every activity at the firm, it was crucial in developing pitches and managing deals.

The firm had never managed one technology platform for anything across their network. Multiple platforms made it especially hard for new employees to navigate the company, which hired 40,000 new employees every year, 20,000 of whom came straight out of school. The average age at the firm was 28. The firm wanted them to be at their best from day one, yet it gave them weak tools—millenials were the first generation that had better technology in their back pockets than they had at work.

When the firm interviewed millennials who'd joined and left within 12 months, they shared a common complaint. They told the firm they were frustrated using traditional tools; they wanted business social networking tools that reflected the way they wanted to work.

Implementation

Rather than piloting its social intranet, Spark, the firm launched Spark in April of 2012 with "waves." The firm positioned Spark as bold and new; everyone wanted to be part of the first wave. Employees used iPhones and Skype to contribute to a promotional video. They helped position the system as "the place" to go to connect with colleagues, collaborate, and create value for themselves and their clients. Adoption grew virally until formal launches occurred in each country.

The firm described its business social networking journey as a series of "90-day sprints." The initial post-launch sprint introduced Spark as "above the flow of work." The second adoption sprint focused on bringing Spark "into the flow of work," which involved using Spark for discussions on client matters in a secure manner.

Results

Any time the firm can save time writing a proposal, it responds to clients faster, saves on costs, and bills more hours. It has already started to see improvements in the proposal process. For instance, the firm had only two weeks to turn around a $10 million retail sector proposal. Using Spark, it finished the proposal in only one week. Team members didn't spend time chasing e-mails and documents. By collaborating online they reduced version control issues by 80 percent. Soon the firm was seeing returns of 80 percent cost savings in developing new proposals.

Prior to Spark, the firm used traditional knowledge management tools to gather best practices, methodologies, and precedent materials. The information was codified, organized and edited. Spark brings this knowledge to life in an environment full of conversations, interactions, experiences, connections, tips, and advice.

Additional Wins

While Spark was a great tool for deal management, the firm introduced it across the company for a multitude of purposes. One firm partner can list numerous ways that Spark has changed how it does business:

▶ In March 2012, the Canadian government released several amendments to its budget. The changes would affect U.S. companies that invested in the country. The release occurred at noon, but by the end of the afternoon, the Canadian tax partners had already put their thoughts together and posted them on Spark. The U.S. partners picked it up that evening and, saw it would impact their clients' inbound investments. When the U.S. partners called their clients the next morning, clients that were accustomed to a longer turnaround were blown away.

▶ Messages travel around the world on Spark. A financial services manager in Germany was working on a large insurance company account and needed expertise in Open Pages (governance, risk, and compliance software). He put a request out on Spark and, in two minutes, an employee in London noted the entry. He used @mentioning to discuss this issue with several technology groups. An employee based in New York suggested an OpenPages expert in San Francisco who then gave names of four people in Germany who could help the original manager in Germany. Conversations pinged across the firm's network, and, in 26 minutes, the manager got an answer to his question.

In early 2013, over half of the firm's 180,000 employees were already engaged on the system. Now the firm is looking into how to use it to connect with the firm's alumni and clients. For a company whose future depends on recruiting young professionals, a social intranet is the perfect solution. As the company's global head of knowledge management boasts, "It works, it's intuitive, it's social—it's not a clunky, typical enterprise tool. It's modern and represents the modern way of working."

Sales Enablement

Value Proposition

Sales enablement is the process of getting the salespeople what they need—product specifications, names of decision makers, performance statistics, etc.—to make their quota and, ultimately, be successful in their jobs. When companies use a social platform for sales enablement, they can train and onboard new sales representatives more quickly, reduce the load on trainers and coaches, and develop marketing collateral faster. The faster enterprises get salespeople up to speed, the sooner new representatives start closing deals. When sales representatives can "self-help" by easily locating documents and resources and reusing existing knowledge, they save time and start generating revenue immediately.

Using a social business platform, organizations reduce sales support needs by 14 percent. They develop marketing collateral 28 percent faster than before and can reduce the time it takes to onboard new reps by 23 percent. Finally, sales rep turnover falls because sales reps are more successful, less frustrated, and more connected to their team. This leads to a 1 to 2 percent increase in total revenue.

Flow: Onboarding

Onboarding—the process of taking new employees and making them revenue producers—involves several people in the sales team from training managers, training coordinators, sales coaches and leaders, to, finally, the new sales hire. Trainers develop the sales tools for new hires, while the coordinators set the sessions schedule, make travel plans, and ensure new hires read the preview material. After the training, the training manager and coaches gather feedback on the sessions. On-the-job training then continues past this point in perpetuity.

Pain Points: Onboarding

While straightforward, onboarding is an expensive and time-consuming process for both the trainers and the new hires. Training managers gather content from across many silos, but they get no feedback as to how new salespeople and coaches actually use the material in the field. Logistical issues like scheduling can bog down the process and add expense.

New hires are eager to get going. Required training feels like a necessary evil and a stumbling block for quota-generating activities. When training finishes, trainers get limited feedback on the sessions and it's difficult to maintain the community for continuous learning.

Figures 4.2 and 4.2A outline the sales onboarding process and the common pain points.

Flow: Sales Support

Sales representatives begin by qualifying leads. Reps use product and industry information to learn about the product, industry, and customers. Then, with the help of other sales representatives, they match current opportunities with deals arranged in the past

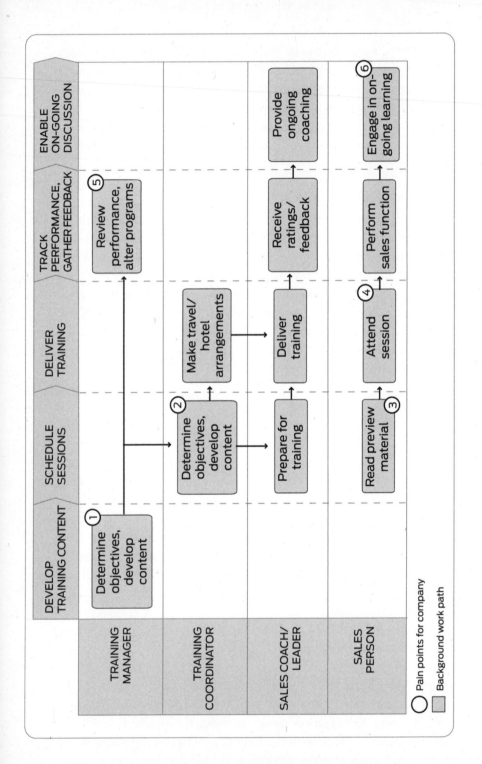

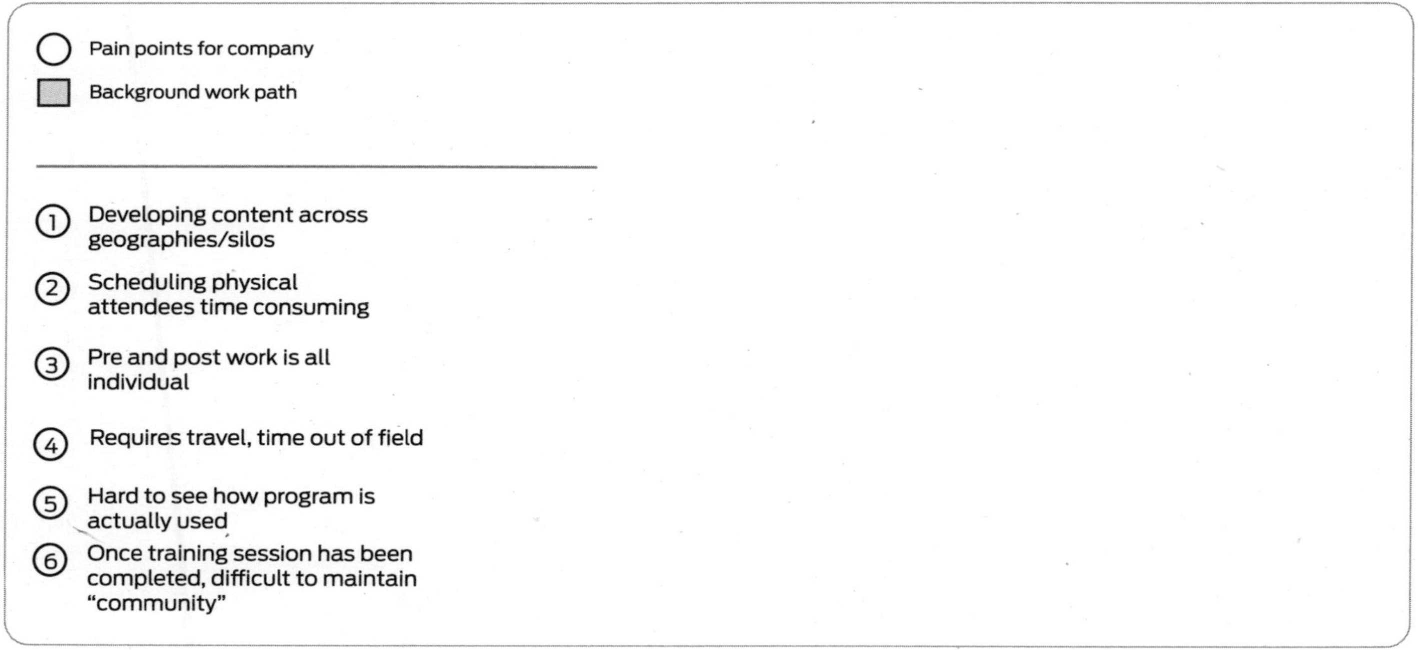

Pain points for company

Background work path

1. Developing content across geographies/silos

2. Scheduling physical attendees time consuming

3. Pre and post work is all individual

4. Requires travel, time out of field

5. Hard to see how program is actually used

6. Once training session has been completed, difficult to maintain "community"

FIGURES 4.2 AND 4.2A. Sales Enablement Process and Pain Points (Onboarding) to try to leverage any previous sales experience. The next step is to pitch, negotiate, and close the deal. Once they make the sale, they update deal information and capture what they learn.

Pain Points: Sales Support

Much of the sales support process involves creating and managing sales collateral and reference material. It's difficult to keep the most current versions of documents up-to-date. Even when they are timely, it's hard to find them. Content developers crave feedback from salespeople, marketing, and training personnel, but finding the time to exchange informal and formal feedback is a challenge.

Because it's too hard to e-mail files around to everyone, most sales and marketing departments develop content in their silo. This makes it hard for salespeople to know what the best content is and where to find it; sales collateral ends up in e-mails or on intranets that are difficult to query. When it comes time to develop a proposal, gathering feedback poses the same problems. Finally, much of the information about sales leads goes undocumented, which translates to lost sales and slower sales cycles. Figures 4.3 and 4.3A outline the process of providing sales support and the shortcomings of the current process.

Case Study: Devoteam

Devoteam, a French ICT consulting firm with more than 4,700 employees across Europe and the Middle East, wanted to close sales faster and win more of the deals they pitched. Two factors made the selling process complicated: Devoteam had recently made several acquisitions and Devoteam's offering had gotten more complex. The company was transitioning from a professional services model—sending consultants as contractors to client sites—to a solution model where they provided large-scale, end-to-end technology solutions. To sell the new projects, Devoteam had to write more complex proposals. They needed to get several groups in the company to collaborate—sales, engineering, consulting, and legal—which meant that getting out an RFP took progressively longer. This put Devoteam even further away from revenue as it tripled the sales cycle from three to nine months.

To stay competitive even as sales grew more complicated, Devoteam needed new tools. They still relied on e-mail, phone calls, and face-to-face meetings. Devoteam had several pain points that they hoped a social business platform could address:

Prioritization: Devoteam wasn't convinced they were only going after the best deals, yet they invested more in assembling RFPs. This pushed the stakes higher and the opportunity costs of going after the wrong deals higher too.

Coordination: Bringing together members from across the company (different regions, departments) to understand customer needs, write a proposal, approve and negotiate a deal became an immense challenge.

Multiple meetings: Employees were taking part in hundreds of meetings per year at every stage of the sales process. This was time consuming and expensive.

Document management: Sales and product-related documents were scattered over e-mail and on laptops. Tracking documents and maintaining version control was a challenge, as was collecting and building upon best practices/past successes.

"It was an unsustainable situation," according to Nicolas Morlière, head of bid development at Devoteam. "We had to find a way to get more consistent, unified, and agile, and better leverage our people." Devoteam needed a tool that could support the company's new sales process and enforce procedures, but be flexible enough to work across any deal or situation. And it also had to be easy to use. The company was adamant that employees wouldn't need formal training before they used the platform.[13]

Implementation

Devoteam chose a hosted (cloud) solution, implemented it quickly, and got it fully functional in only eight weeks. The social business platform became the hub for sales at Devoteam. No matter where employees were physically located around Europe, they could easily come together to create and review pitches and other

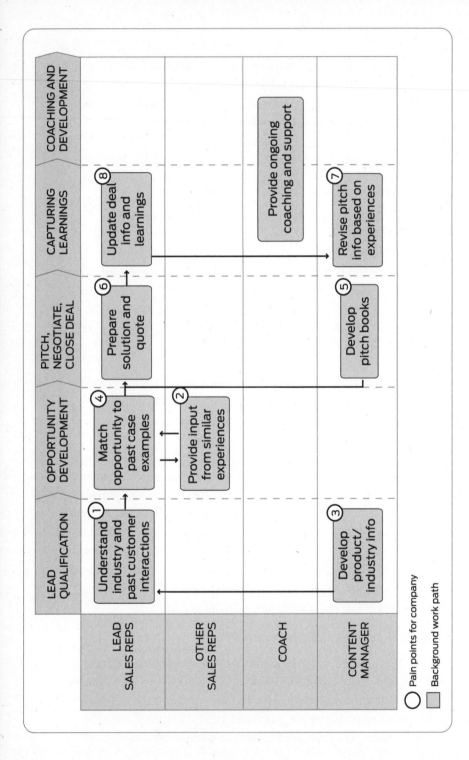

○ Pain points for company

■ Background work path

① Sales enablement docs/tools hard to find/prioritize

② Difficult to discuss opportunities and ideas across phyical boundaries

③ Hard/slow to develop across silos with marketing and product

④ Case history not up to date, and lots of color not available in CRM tool

⑤ Hard/slow to develop across silos with sales ops

⑥ Coordinating on solution pitch, approvals, negotiations can be slow

⑦ No strong feedback loop on sales enablement documents/info

⑧ Difficult/time consuming to capture learning to update documentation, customer profile, etc.

FIGURES 4.3 AND 4.3A. Sales Enablement Process Pain Points (Sales Support)

documents, locate experts, get answers to crucial questions, and update each other via smart activity streams.

Everyone at Devoteam who was involved in advanced solution selling—more than 400 sales, sales support, technical sales, and sales management personnel—used the social intranet to track internal sales activities for complex deals. They used the platform for each step of the sales process: assembling the investment request and materials (plus getting approval), building the proposal, managing the negotiation/response, and closing the deal. The social platform documented each step and marked it with a status. In 2012, they completed several hundred deals and generated more than $500 million.

The social platform offered increased value, yet salespeople had to do little additional work to benefit from it. Each step had its own pre-defined templates on the platform to ensure that sales representatives thoroughly collected the required information. Once a sale passed the investment decision, the sale became a "project" on the platform. Then, when the sales lead found appropriate experts/participants through the social business platform, the lead invited them to participate in the project. Teams launched virtual deal rooms—a single place to collaborate around a specific sale opportunity. In the deal room, reps could meet sales support experts and find competitive materials, RFPs and proposal documents, pitch decks, customer questions, CRM opportunity data and more. Sales materials, best practices, and other information were all available on the social business platform to help new reps come up to speed and prepare a proposal.

The social platform also created a stronger connection between sales and marketing, again without giving either team new work. Every time that a salesperson presented a pitch deck to a prospect via the iPad, an automatic notification went to the corporate marketing team. The rep didn't comment on the deck s/he used with a prospect—i.e., explain what worked and what didn't. Automatically, the marketing team learned which marketing collateral the rep used, even how much time the rep spent on each slide. Finally, marketing was able to close the loop with the sales team and get them exactly the information they needed.

Sales Enablement on a Social Business Platform vs. Salesforce.com

Some sales organizations worry that they can't introduce another tool to sales. Managers can see that reps already have trouble keeping up with data entry on Salesforce.com or another CRM system.

One problem with CRM software is that the sales team is usually the only group that uses it. Marketing, pricing, and product management—they aren't on the system. A social business platform reaches beyond salespeople to include everyone who is part of the sales process. When all of these teams are engaged on one system, the rep doesn't have to spend time looking for the latest sales presentation, finding the right pricing expert to verify a new offer, or contacts at the prospect. In return, the marketing and product management teams can get automatic updates on the quality and utility of marketing materials while remaining in direct contact with the people on the front lines.

A social business platform can make a new sales rep's first contact with an existing customer more favorable. Without much context or information from a previous sales representative, new reps can't know each customer's issues. For a new salesperson, each account represents quota relief. The more a rep can know, the more likely it is for them to make a sale.

Companies evaluating a social business platform also wonder about reps' incentives to collaborate. They ask, "What if the top performers don't want to share their experience and ideas?" We've seen that once a rep experiences how easy it is to get answers from colleagues, they want to make their own ideas available too.

Results

The social business platform has brought standardization and transparency to Devoteam's sales process. By working more efficiently, Devoteam has shrunk sales costs by $1.5 million annually. Deal cycles times are 30 percent shorter, sales support costs are 29 percent lower, and sales onboarding time has fallen from one month to only two weeks.

The net revenue impact is an increase in sales of $4 to $5 million and a 33 percent higher win rate, in-line with industry leaders. Finally, the company has greater management visibility into the sales funnel and process.

The social business platform has improved both the speed and the quality of Devoteam's proposals. According to Elise Bruchet, head of marketing and social business, "The sales community has successfully adopted this new way of working; making collaboration and information sharing key to our sales tactics. We better understand and respond to customer needs and avoid missed opportunities because of lack of transparency and information locked in someone's mailbox."

Marketing Design and Execution

Value Proposition

A social business platform helps companies develop marketing collateral, launch campaigns faster, and make marketing campaigns more effective. Traditionally, this work involves a lot of team coordination, scheduling, and planning. When a company uses a social tool to develop marketing materials, they can focus just on the quality of the materials they produce. Instead of relying on e-mail, conference calls, or meetings, the social platform serves as a virtual meeting place; the platform becomes the destination for marketing and customer interaction.

Firms are able to develop marketing collateral 28 percent faster by working collaboratively across marketing, sales, and product management. And when they produce better quality material in less time, sales productivity rises by up to 12 percent.

A social business platform also helps marketers develop and launch campaigns faster. Internal marketing teams can coordinate with outside agencies' involvement, collaborate on materials, and distribute content to various channels via the social business platform. By tapping into social media channels outside the company, marketers can easily monitor and engage in real-time feedback on in-market campaigns. This makes the campaigns 10 percent more effective, on average. Marketing teams can develop campaigns faster, which means they can launch more of them. Specifically, a social business platform helps shorten campaign development by 13 percent and companies can launch, on average, 15 percent more campaigns.

When companies can reduce cycle times for collateral development and launch more effective campaigns faster, they improve revenue by 1 to 2 percent.

Flow

Marketing design and execution requires individuals from multiple areas—inside and outside an organization—to coordinate on everything from the design of a campaign to tracking the campaign upon completion. The main steps of the process are determining objectives and writing a brief; designing and developing a campaign; testing, tracking performance, and adjusting deliverables; finalization and launch; and making adjustments once the content is already out in the market.

Pain Points

Marketing departments often have the biggest budget in a company but the smallest staff. They have to be able to work across a firewall since many of their collaborators are external contractors or agencies. While they can set up files in the cloud, working with outsiders is more complicated than staying inside the corporate firewall.

What's difficult about campaign development and management is getting all participants—product management, product/corporate marketing, external creative agencies, marketing analytics, and public relations/corporate communications—together. If they were only able to communicate on a shared platform, the process of creating material or planning a conference, gathering feedback, and getting approvals could be done quickly and easily.

Figures 4.4 and 4.4A, 4.5 and 4.5A, and 4.6 and 4.6A point out the flow and pain points of developing marketing collateral, planning events, and launching campaigns.

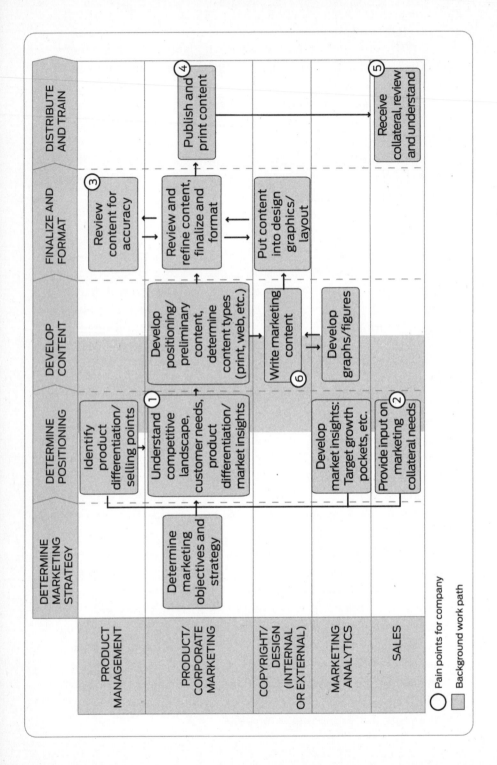

118

○ Pain points for company

▪ Background work path

① Difficult to collect and synthesize information and insights

② Sales oftentimes not sufficiently involved

③ Outside department reviews/approvals difficult to coordinate, time consuming

④ Marketing collateral oftentimes not properly coordinated with launch (too late, etc.)

⑤ Collateral posted to an intranet, hard to find the right information; feedback loop to marketing very slow

⑥ Coordinating content development/version control/difficult, slow, time consuming

FIGURES 4.4 AND 4.4A. Marketing Material/Collateral Development Pain Points

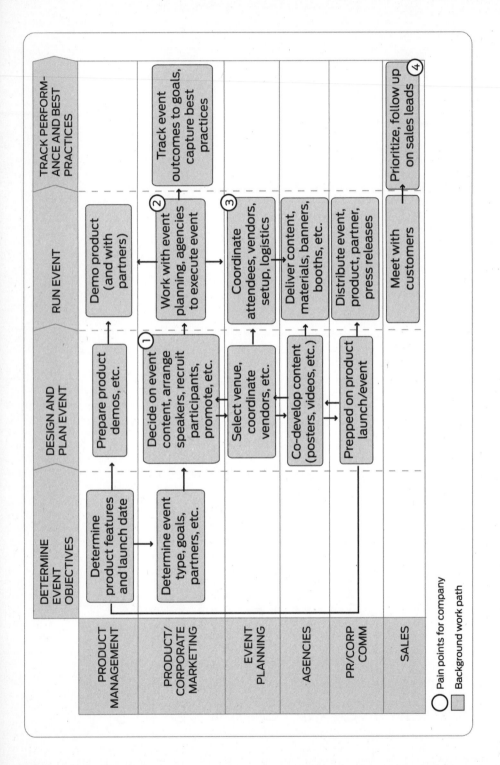

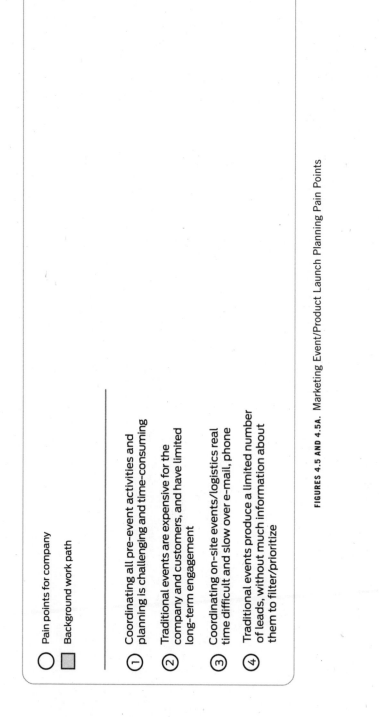

○ Pain points for company

▢ Background work path

① Coordinating all pre-event activities and planning is challenging and time-consuming

② Traditional events are expensive for the company and customers, and have limited long-term engagement

③ Coordinating on-site events/logistics real time difficult and slow over e-mail, phone

④ Traditional events produce a limited number of leads, without much information about them to filter/prioritize

FIGURES 4.5 AND 4.5A. Marketing Event/Product Launch Planning Pain Points

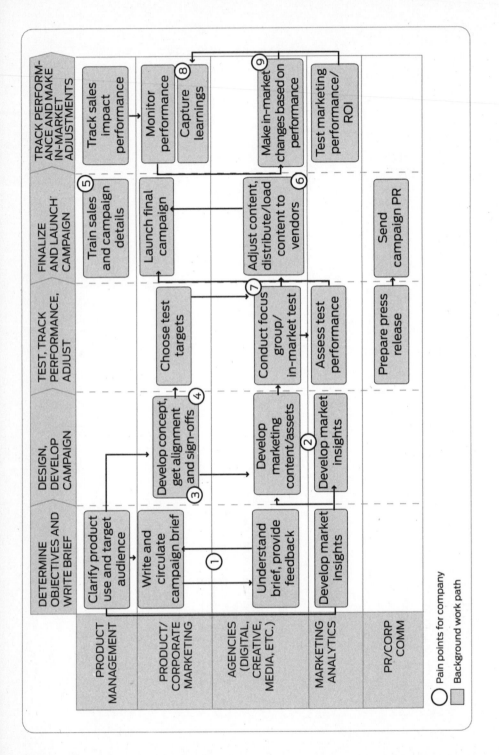

○ Pain points for company

▨ Background work path

① Diffcult to get all parties (internal and external) aligned on brief

② Challenging to share assets and collaborate across various agencies

③ Hard to get necessary approvals and sign-offs

④ Difficult for different internal marketing departments to coordinate (e.g., avoid media competition)

⑤ Difficult to keep sales up to date on campaign and give real-time in-market input to marketing

⑥ Difficult to coordinate content distribution to all vendors/partners

⑦ Challenging to manage tests, share insights, and determine next steps

⑧ Difficult to capture/codify lessons learned

⑨ Hard to communicate with all parties to share performance and align on adjustments

FIGURES 4.6 AND 4.6A. Marketing Campaign Development Pain Points

Case Study: EMC

In 2010, EMC had to navigate an uncertain economy and a flat corporate marketing budget. It was the classic "do more with less" conundrum. EMC had a global marketing team of 1,400 employees and was a $21 billion leader in global business systems. But considering the financial climate, it needed to become more efficient. EMC already used several social technologies, but not in any systematic way. Jeremy Burton, EMC's chief marketing officer, believed that the global marketing team could use social to create stronger relationships with customers.

Burton was confident that if EMC marketers could easily interact with prospects, customers, and partners without the friction of conference calls, cost of pilot tests, and lengthy content development, they'd be able to improve marketing ROI.

The social platform needed rich social features and had to be scalable to the entire enterprise and beyond. But simplicity and design were also critical—EMC would only be able to give users limited support.

Implementation

EMC launched both external and internal social communities for marketing management and execution. (The external community, ECN, used a cloud platform while the internal community ran on on-premise software.) EMC completely transitioned all marketing activities to the social business platform.

The internal community became the open workspace for campaign planning and management and everything that went along with product launches, including live event planning and an online launch.

Customers visited the external community and learned about new and existing products. EMC could meet customers directly without the hassle of meetings and collaborate with them in a manner that mirrored how they acted in their personal lives. EMC also used gamification—contests and badges—to intertwine online and offline experiences (e.g., customers who visited EMC's booth at the VM World conference earned 10 points, which then appeared on their profile page on the social intranet) and increase engagement.

EMC could be "in the room" when customers talked to each other on the platform. Even if EMC wasn't directly talking to customers, the conversations took place under EMC's control. This gave EMC a direct line to customer needs/wants and demand patterns.

Impact: External Community

EMC's external community for its 256,000 customers, EMC Community Network (ECN), became the first stop for individuals evaluating EMC products: 50 percent of influencers and decision makers go to the external community to learn about EMC products. When EMC performed an analysis on its external community, it found that EMC community members purchased more than non–community members. In fact, in 2012, EMC community members, on average, spent 240 percent more than non–community members (on EMC products and services). As the number of users in a community increases, the average purchase size increases logarithmically.

EMC has had over 170 million conversations (across the complete social ecosystem, including both Twitter and Facebook) in two years since the launch. These include customer conversations, issue resolutions, and suggestions across ECN and other social platforms. According to Burton, "We simply couldn't have had that many conversations with our customers at any cost over e-mail and the phone." EMC provides better service and, ultimately, has gained a competitive advantage over its peers.

Brace Rennels, director of community strategy, likens the corporate purchase process to a consumer e-commerce experience:

> First, we search the Internet for a product we need—for instance, a camera. Once we identify a possible solution, we want to validate the potential purchase. We look to others or "peers" who may have already purchased that camera and/ or have written a review. Once we've made a selection, we look for accessories that peers suggest we buy to go along with that camera: a tripod, lens cleaners, case, batteries or larger memory card. Suddenly, the original camera purchase just became more expensive.

In 2012, EMC launched eight products within six months solely in the ECN community. It expanded the awareness/visibility of its products by upwards of 50 percent. Again, because the content lives on the community, it's available to customers 24/7. The original eight launches have now generated 80,000 page views, a number that continues to grow every day as users more frequently return to the site.

Impact: Internal Community

ECN has changed the way EMC launches products and has reduced much of the friction in running a campaign. Instead of a mishmash of phone calls, e-mail, web conferences, and focus groups, everything happens on the social business platform. EMC's 1,400 marketing employees can concentrate on getting the best ideas out to customers and prospects—not managing calendars and planning meetings. The platform also facilitates communication with regional marketing bodies. When EMC created a global campaign that required localization, it could quickly get feedback from regions.

As an added bonus, both vendors and EMC employees have started to use the internal community as a one-stop shop for global marketing guidelines, policies, scheduling, and resources. The platform works side-by-side with a host of third-party solutions: marketing automation, web platform, customer/ROI tracking, Salesforce.com, and digital asset management. Integration is easy.

Premier Farnell

Premier Farnell is a global distributor of electronic components for engineers. Similar to EMC, the company had an e-commerce site but wanted to improve marketing ROI. Accordingly, it launched a customer community—element14—for social commerce, social marketing, and customer support for its global engineering community.

Prior to the launch, many people in the company doubted that engineers would engage on an online community. It turned out, however, that engineers find it helpful to talk to peers before making a purchase decision. They want to share new ideas, challenges, and technical issues.

element14 connects seamlessly to Premier Farnell's e-commerce site. Whenever a user mentions a product on the site, element14 automatically turns it into a link to that product and related products.

Users can also see a "quick view" with a region-specific price, availability, and technical documentation. Members click to purchase, add a product to a list of things to purchase later, or e-mail the information to a colleague.

When engineers log on to element14, they get access to the industry's latest products from leading manufacturers and sign up to test and review products for free. element14 sends these reviews back to manufacturers to help them improve their offering.

Three years post-launch, element14 had over 115,000 registered members, with a 60 percent annual growth rate in monthly participation. In 2012, over 5 percent of customers clicked through to purchase, and then 18 percent of them converted from browsers to buyers. This is four times the conversion rate of Premier Farnell's typical e-commerce customer. The community also is a draw to prospective customers. Approximately 50 percent of visitors to element14 are new to Premier Farnell.

Today, element14 is an integral part of company strategy and how Premier Farnell acquires and manages its customers. element14 is one of the company's fastest-growing go-to-market channels in sales. As Nicole Fusz, community manager, suggests, customers are actually reducing the cost of sales: "We've created cheerleaders for our brand. When someone has an issue, the community rallies and stands up for us."

Customer Service
Value Proposition

We all have experienced it. Companies don't always offer the level of service that customers want. We want simple solutions to our problems and, increasingly, we want them faster. Once, customers used to send in a complaint or question by mail. Then they started calling the consumer helpline, accessing a website, initiating a live chat program, and, finally, engaging in interactive customer service. Every new communication technology has demonstrated to customers that answers will come increasingly fast.

What customers really want is to dispense with customer service altogether. They need tools for self-service. They're tired of explaining a problem to one customer service representative, getting transferred to another representative, repeating the story, then finally connecting to the subject matter expert who may or may not be able to solve the problem. They'd also like a way to connect with other customers that have dealt with the same problem, learn how those customers solved the problem, and then try solving it themselves.

When companies use a social platform in customer service, especially customer self-service, fewer calls go to agents. Customers can get the answers they need by querying a robust knowledge base the first time they call. Overall call volume falls by 8 percent and the number of problems that the company resolves on the first call increases by 16 percent. When calls do reach customer service representatives, employees tap the external and internal support communities to find better answers to customer questions.

Companies using social business platforms for customer service have experienced a 15 percent drop in handle time (length of calls) and a 13 percent decrease in calls escalated to managers. These changes push total customer service costs down by 9 percent.

Additionally, social customer service improves customer satisfaction and increases recurring revenue. When representatives work on more interesting issues and can contribute to solving a problem, they are more likely to stay at the company. Lower turnover means that customers reach more experienced representatives and the company saves money. Finally, a social platform makes it easy to provide real-time feedback to the product group on customer issues so that product managers and engineers can resolve those issues faster.

Flow

In most firms, the customer service process involves four steps: problem occurrence and self-assessment, issue triage and problem identification, issue resolution, and issue close and resolution documentation. Depending on the problem, this process might include everyone from a single customer to two tiers of customer support.

When customers have issues, they usually start with the vendor's online knowledge base or FAQs. If they can't solve the problem on their own, they contact customer support through the phone or web. The support representative searches the knowledge base for a resolution. He or she reaches out to colleagues for help, works with a supervisor who might have more experience, and might also call on other experts. Once the team finds a solution, they communicate it to the customer and loop back to the content development team to update the knowledge base. The customer service representative then offers the solution to the customer, who implements the fix and tests the product.

In the background, the content development and product management teams are continuously testing new products and writing manuals and other documentation with the help of the product management team. The customer service representatives take this documentation and use it to learn about new and existing products.

Pain Points

Today's content tools—websites, forms, and FAQs—are not keeping up with the pace of change. Increasing product complexity and the constant need to update the product knowledge base make customer service a frustrating job. Customer service representatives in call centers spend their days answering questions and getting yelled at by frustrated customers. They communicate with the external world and other coworkers in customer service. They lack visibility into other parts of the company. They don't know about big product launches or the issues that marketing, sales, product development, finance, IT, or any other department are facing.

When companies could predict the questions that customers would ask, technologies like forms and FAQs were a defensive barrier for companies to keep customers from taking too much support time. But when product sophistication increases at lightning speed, the product management team can't write new product manuals to keep up with the speed of innovation. Companies struggle to get the right information to content development and then to customer support representatives and customers. When customers contact the support team, representatives can't solve their problem, even with the help of a colleague. Frontline representatives escalate more questions, and customer service expenses grow.

The other cost is employee turnover. Representatives don't feel empowered in their jobs. Further, due to the lack of a simple feedback cycle and real-time product feedback, serious customer issues can take days or weeks to get noticed.

Figures 4.7 and 4.7A outline the customer service process and highlight the pain points common to many customer service organizations.

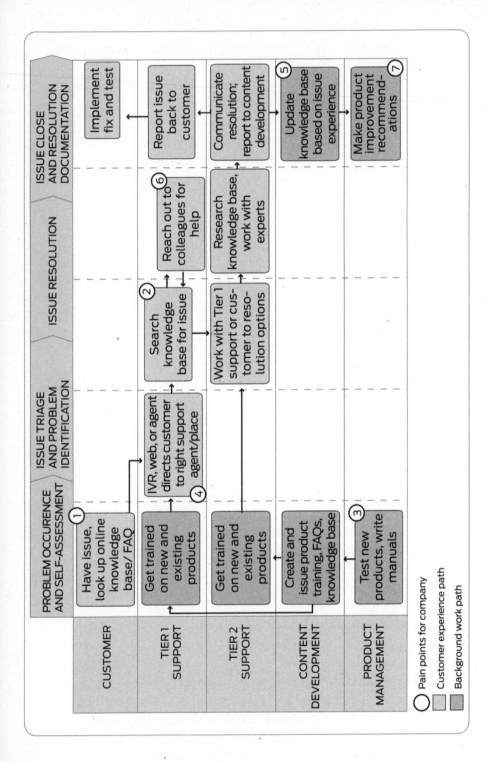

PROBLEM OCCURRENCE AND SELF-ASSESSMENT | ISSUE TRIAGE AND PROBLEM IDENTIFICATION | ISSUE RESOLUTION | ISSUE CLOSE AND RESOLUTION DOCUMENTATION

CUSTOMER
- ① Have issue, look up online knowledge base/ FAQ
- Report issue back to customer

TIER 1 SUPPORT
- Get trained on new and existing products
- ④ IVR, web, or agent directs customer to right support agent/place
- ② Search knowledge base for issue
- ⑥ Reach out to colleagues for help
- Implement fix and test

TIER 2 SUPPORT
- Get trained on new and existing products
- Work with Tier 1 support or customer to resolution options
- Research knowledge base, work with experts
- Communicate resolution; report to content development

CONTENT DEVELOPMENT
- Create and issue product training, FAQs, knowledge base
- ⑤ Update knowledge base based on issue experience

PRODUCT MANAGEMENT
- ③ Test new products, write manuals
- ⑦ Make product improvement recommendations

Legend:
- ◯ Pain points for company
- Customer experience path
- Background work path

Pain points for company

Customer experience path

Background work path

① Knowledge base is only updated periodically by vendor, not always relevant

② Tier 1 reps handling lots of low-level issues, causes low job engagement/ excitement

③ Increasing product complexity and shorter rev cycles make training more difficult

④ Customer can't self-resolve, phone support expensive and offers poor experience

⑤ ~30 day cycle to update knowledge base

⑥ Knowledge limited to agent experience or that of "next door" colleague; increases call escalations

⑦ Difficult to get real-time feedback on product issues/performance

FIGURES 4.7 AND 4.7A. Customer Service Process Pain Points

Case Study: McAfee

McAfee, the world's largest dedicated security company, believed customer support could differentiate it from its competitors. In 2009, it wanted to turn business-to-business customer service from a cost center to a revenue driver. However, with 7,500 employees serving 125 million customers globally, the transition would be a monumental task.

McAfee needed access to customer conversations. Customers communicated in external communities, but McAfee was on the outside looking in; the company could not monitor or participate in these conversations. Its existing infrastructure, particularly a homegrown website, wasn't scalable to include McAfee in these discussions.

McAfee was moving away from antivirus and into comprehensive solutions (e.g., host intrusion, forensics, etc.). The company had to support over 100 products on multiple platforms—mobile, tablet, desktop, etc. It was hard for reps to keep up with all the products and correctly answer customers' questions.

Implementation

It took only five months, including all customizations, data migration, and testing, for McAfee to set up both an external community for customers and an internal community for customer service representatives.

These communities hosted a variety of support resources ranging from knowledge bases to videos and blog posts. Instead of users aimlessly trolling the site, the tool's social intelligence could surface the best responses in discussions, recommend relevant content, and quickly point users to the people and information who could best help them. McAfee's external community is peer to peer, but support representatives often participate, helping customers resolve problems and engage in conversations that result in valuable product feedback.

Impact

McAfee's social business platform implementations contributed to direct cost savings: McAfee's calls costs declined by $2.6 million annually. Customers found answers to their questions without involving customer service. Self-service meant that 26 percent fewer calls reached customer service. Even as the number of customers grew by 5 percent, support reps provided 3.1 percent fewer minutes of service.

By 2012, McAfee was saving $350,000 annually, from lower employee and IT costs and from shutting down legacy systems. Employee turnover fell by 10 percent, onboarding time declined 50 percent, and IT spending fell by 5 percent.

IDC now rates McAfee among the top companies in customer service. The external support community has over 2.6 million unique visitors annually, 100,000 registered users, and is growing. A majority (58 percent) of customers are able to solve their own problems in the support community. When customers do reach a McAfee representative, the rep is able to resolve the problem in one call 17 percent more frequently. As an added bonus, the external community has become a rich, self-sustaining external group where users are helping each other.

When customers have a better experience with McAfee support, they are more satisfied with the company and more likely to renew their subscription. To wit, McAfee has experienced a 25 percent increase in customer satisfaction and a 33 percent increase in loyalty.

A larger percentage of McAfee employees, 1,000 individuals, regularly participate on the internal platform. Some of the internal community's heaviest users are 150 customer support representatives who access it for issue resolution, collaboration, and idea sharing. They can even pull in discussions from the customer community and work together to rapidly resolve these tough customer cases.

New representatives can get up to speed quickly by spending time on the community. In fact, McAfee has been able to cut the onboarding process by 50 percent (from six months to three months). The platform even impacts job satisfaction. McAfee employees feel better about their jobs because they are working on more advanced customer cases and can actively participate in a community with customers and colleagues.

Case Study: T-Mobile

T-Mobile and MetroPCS became TMUS on the New York Stock Exchange on May 1, 2013. Together, they are the nation's fourth largest wireless provider, serving more than 42 million subscribers with their nationwide 4G network and about 70,000 total points of distribution. In an extremely competitive industry, T-Mobile knew it had to work smarter and faster. It chose to differentiate itself by great customer service.

Typically, people who walk into a T-Mobile retail outlet either want troubleshooting help ("Why doesn't my device do X?") or wish to evaluate and purchase a product or service. T-Mobile wanted to cut down the time retail employees spent on trouble-shooting; retail sales representatives could log into as many as eight different systems to find the information they needed. The more time retail employees spent troubleshooting issues, the less time they spent selling devices and services. But if they sacrificed service for sales, they hurt sales in the long run.

To add to this challenge, employees had no unified voice when they talked to customers. According to Scott Tweedy, vice president of customer experience:

> We had the warring tribes of T-Mobile. A customer service rep in a call center would say something to a customer from a document, but the rep in a retail store would say something else. There was no "one version of the truth"; we had no consistency across the channels.[14]

One reason reps were inconsistent was that they didn't get accurate and timely information. Creating content for T-Mobile employees was too complex. T-Mobile had a 36-step publishing process for every product, rate plan, or other change it introduced. Nine different teams had to the touch content before it was published.

T-Mobile knew it had a problem. The T-Mobile products that employees were selling and/or supporting were becoming more complicated by the day, but the information-sharing process relied on outdated systems. The company's growth would stall if it couldn't evolve its knowledge sharing platforms. As Will Rose, T-Community manager, explained, "We couldn't keep pace with the speed of technology."[15]

Implementation

T-Mobile's strategy with its social business platform, T-Community, was to connect the dots between customer care operations, B2B operations, and retail sales. T-Mobile consolidated and centralized the information about products, services, pricing, troubleshooting—everything that pertained to the front line of its business—onto T-Community.

Now when T-Mobile launches a new product and encounters a software glitch, it no longer has to identify an issue, go back to product management, and then communicate to customers and staff with a resolution. Instead, it just puts the information on T-Community and the right people see the information and act.

Impact

With T-Community, T-Mobile achieved three primary objectives for its retail business:

- ▶ Arm its field sales reps with the right answer, fast
- ▶ Provide better support for a consultative sale
- ▶ Speed up customer "onboarding" without sacrificing service

For T-Mobile's product management and content teams, content development became far simpler. It went from 21 days to a two-step process taking less than a day. T-Mobile also uses T-Community to address questions about processes and business issues and for training.

T-Mobile reported that support representatives' knowledge scores went up 30 percent because of increased knowledge sharing on T-Community. With better-informed support representatives, T-Mobile has seen a 2 percent reduction in issues requiring escalation. Conservatively, this 2 percent improvement equates to millions of operational savings per year.

In call centers, T-Mobile has made significant gains in call resolution time, CRT. Globally, the annual cost of resolving calls with
customers is approximately $2.5 million per second. With a social
business platform, T-Mobile has been able to make a three- to four-
second reduction in CRT, equating to $7.5 million savings per year.

T-Mobile has also slashed publishing expenses. It had been
spending $1 million annually for one system alone. Using a social
business platform, T-Mobile could retire that system, retire 14 other
systems, and reduce the publishing staff by 50 percent—head
count in the department has fallen from 80 people to 40 people.

PAIN ALLEVIATION IMPLEMENTATIONS

Instead of introducing a social platform to an entire company
or business unit, sometimes it makes sense to roll it out first to a
workgroup. Groups that get the most benefit from social business
platforms typically have the following characteristics:

- The entire team is geographically dispersed, or a portion
  of the team operates mainly in the field and rarely comes
  onsite.
- Time or work cycle differences make real-time communication
  between team members a challenge.
- Individuals perform a repeatable, persistent activity rather
  than a project requiring a high level of team-oriented work.
- High velocity—constant tag in/tag out or onboarding—of
  team members makes maintaining context critical.
- Everyone in the group has visibility to the communication
  for both the workgroup and the enterprise as a whole.
- The team or workgroup experiences a certain level of pain
  using existing tools.

While almost any workgroup will benefit from a better communications tool, the more times you can check the box on the items

above, the more likely you'll find a good fit. A small team needs to have more pain than a larger one if implementation is going to be successful. Two examples of workgroups that can benefit from social business platforms are crisis management and distribution management.

Crisis management is about solving urgent problems. Whether it's the collapse of the U.S. banking system, the BP oil spill in the Gulf of Mexico, or the Tylenol cyanide tampering, what often delays a resolution is finding the right people, getting them together, and gathering feedback from anyone touched by the problem. Social business platforms help get people together quickly to resolve a situation efficiently.

A large retailer might run several distribution centers that coordinate inventory levels so that the right merchandise reaches the customers who need it most. There's no magic number of employees required to get the job done. Target, the discount retailer, only has four food distribution centers (it operates 37 general distribution centers). Regardless of the number of centers, though, a workgroup made up of four distribution center managers will find value in using a social business platform to manage inventory across the company.

Workgroups look to a social business platform not for specific business value but because they want to alleviate pain. They are trying to do a specific job and don't have the tools to do it. These teams ultimately anchor a social business platform initiative within (or as predecessor to) an enterprise rollout because the tools they have don't do the job. These teams can make a quick purchase decision because they don't require coordination with the rest of the organization.

A social business platform won't be valuable to every workgroup. A development team where all members sit next to each other, have worked together for five years, and communicate easily will get little benefit from a social platform. But for groups that have a persistent function with employees distributed around a company, country, or even the world, a social platform will be a lifeline. These workgroups will get tremendous value from social technologies, even without all of the employees in a company or even a department participating.

Case Study: Health Fitness

Health Fitness is a professional services firm that manages corporate wellness programs and onsite fitness centers; one in five Fortune 500 companies is a Health Fitness customer. Health Fitness associates work at the client site independently or as part of a Health Fitness team. Often associates are so integrated into the host company that they are seen as coworkers.

Health Fitness's issue was that associates at client sites around the country effectively did the same job but had no means to connect to one another. Distance and work cycle differences made associates feel more like sole practitioners than members of a team.

As Andrea Bredow, community manager at Health Fitness, recalled, even e-mailing colleagues was difficult because all of the associates used their clients' e-mail domains:

> If an associate had a question, she'd e-mail her boss. The boss would then forward the question to each of his or her direct reports in the field and, in some cases, get a reply-all message back. It could take days to get an answer even to a simple request.

Reaching everyone through the Health Fitness e-mail system was too time-consuming and frustrating since most employee used only their host company's e-mail system.

Associates also struggled to keep abreast of developments at the corporate office. Corporate communications could send mass e-mails, but employees couldn't have a conversation by responding to one of those e-mails. Beyond regional managers' monthly conference calls, associates had few other opportunities to connect with their peers.

Rollout

Health Fitness introduced its social platform, known as Fuser, in mid-2012. (The term "fuser" came from Heath Fitness's mantra, "Infusing a culture of health.") The first users were onsite screeners—employees that did biometric testing at client sites—and also invited the executive team in order to gain their buy-in. After the first 60 days, Health Fitness opened the platform to everyone at the company who worked over 20 hours a week: 1,300 employees.

Results

Fuser was a lifeline for associates who had felt isolated. One associate in Montana, for instance, covered the entire state. On Fuser, she could easily throw out questions to her peers. They not only served as a virtual sounding board but also provided information on their own successful programs. For instance, one associate was considering changing the maps she made of walking trails near the office. When she mentioned this on Fuser, five other associates uploaded and shared their programs. "Having access to these other guides," she explained, "really allowed me to beef up my own program."

The program library was one of Fuser's most popular features. Any time associates launched a program, they uploaded all the plans and results to the library. Someone looking to launch a program on heart healthy lifestyles would find that a colleague launched a similar program. The program initiator could take whichever parts she wanted rather than creating everything from scratch.

After eight months, over 73 percent of Health Fitness full-time employees had registered as Fuser users. Fifty percent of these users were active during the last 30 days and 31 percent were participating on the system. Users ranged in age, technological skills, and location around the United States.

Case Study: Hanley Wood

Hanley Wood develops magazines, websites, e-newsletters, exhibitions and conferences, and custom marketing and data services to serve the residential and commercial construction industries. All magazines are B2B publications and, unlike mass media, serve very specific groups.

Bob Benz, president of content at Hanley Wood, oversaw 27 magazines and 34 e-newsletters and approximately 120 employees across the country. He came to the company as part of Hanley Wood's innovation initiative. When he arrived, the company had recently decided to close all remote offices—Los Angeles, Chicago, and Vermont—and told employees in these offices they'd have to move to Washington, DC, or lose their jobs. Management felt the team would collaborate better if all team members were physically on the same campus.

Benz feared that if he staffed all the magazines out of DC, he wouldn't be able to find the subject-matter expertise he needed. The offices around the country housed writers who were experts in their fields. Chicago concentrated on concrete construction, Los Angeles had pool and spa experts, and Vermont focused on carpenters and remodelers.

Instead of insisting content developers move to DC, Benz found a way for people in these offices to collaborate over long distances. He told his employees, "I won't make you move, but you must become part of our culture." One of the ways to do this was by engaging on a social business platform. Embracing a social platform was also a way for Hanley Wood to become more innovative. As Benz explained, "We are a magazine company that is striving to become multi-platform. Print is diminishing; interactive is ramping up. We need to change the culture. This starts by getting people talking."

Rollout

In June 2012, Hanley Wood introduced Woodworks to a small group of users (many developers were already using it for free) and the CEO. These first users spread the word about Woodworks and recruited their colleagues. While the heaviest users were the content team/editorial groups (120 people), over 500 of all 600 employees enrolled.

When they first launched Woodworks, Benz did a lot of the heavy lifting in terms of getting content on the system. He high-lighted innovative projects that the company was working on and news items such as a journalism award, an editor's promotion, new hires, and even a silly haiku competition. These news items brought users to Woodworks. Then, they started conversing with their coworkers about topics like designing the right product and how to purchase targeted advertisements. According to Benz, "Using Woodworks is not overwhelming. I ask people to start by going on there for 10 minutes a day. That's just a fraction of the time they are spending on Facebook!"

"Unlike e-mail," said Benz, "when you post something on Woodworks, you include a much larger group. People whom you might not have included on an e-mail will add helpful information. Also, it's possible to find valuable information even six months later through a simple search."

Results

Before Woodworks, people who worked on *Pool and Spa News* magazine didn't think they had much in common with writers at the *Journal of Light Construction*. What connected a hot tub installation to a roof? While the specifics for each magazine were different, readers of both magazines struggled with the same issues of running a construction business: getting work permits, disposing of hazardous waste, and acquiring insurance. Once editors of these magazines joined Woodworks, they realized they had much in common. For instance, the teams at the *Journal of Light Construction* in Vermont and *Remodeling* in Washington, DC, might find they are both reviewing power drills. Rather than each of them creating the content, *Remodeling* can do a draft that is more cursory while the *Journal of Light Construction* would do a version that is much more detailed.

Benz explained that coming together on a social business platform is enabling Hanley Wood to do better work more efficiently:

> The more we break silos down, the more efficiently we function and the better we can serve our audiences. We've taken money out of editorial costs while increasing our interactive efforts, and Woodworks definitely played a role.
>
> Web traffic is up, online revenue is growing quickly, our editorial team is collaborating more, and we've moved about a quarter of our staff from print to digital roles with no additional costs. It is game-changing for us. Woodworks feels like our home.

INTRODUCING A SOCIAL BUSINESS PLATFORM TO THE ENTERPRISE

Social Offers Measurable Benefits

According to a top-three management consulting firm, when employees collaborate on a social business platform, they get work done through structured, actionable discussion. They become more productive by reducing their e-mail load by 21 percent and meetings by 16 percent. They locate needed information, expertise, and best practices from across the company 34 percent faster and then use this knowledge to improve quality and innovation. Finally, the workforce becomes aligned with the company's strategic goals. They use the platform to gather feedback to inform the strategy and make better strategic decisions and focus all employees on these strategic priorities.[16]

Figure 4.8 shows the qualitative benefits workers derive from improving collaboration, communication, and access to information.[17]

Information Sharing in Distributed Organizations

In large and/or distributed organizations, employees have difficulty finding the information they need to get their jobs done, even in the presence of a corporate intranet, portal, or knowledge

BENEFITS FOR THE COMPANY	BENEFITS FOR EMPLOYEES
· Increased innovation through the sharing different creation points of view	· Increased access to knowledge, allowing better performance
· Better decision-making/productivity from frontline employees, with better information	· Exposure to a broader group brings job enrichment and engagement
· Revenue increases from expertise and product sharing	· Greater career opportunities and progression
· Cost savings from best-practice transfer	· Reduced frustration from reinventing the wheel and difficulties getting things done

FIGURE 4.8. Benefits to Company and Employees

management system. They inadvertently duplicate their colleagues' work, simply because time and physical distance makes it difficult for them to have an awareness of what others are doing. According to the McKinsey Global Institute, knowledge workers spend nearly 20 percent of their time looking for internal information or tracking down colleagues to assist with specific tasks or projects.[18]

Organizations shift to a remote workforce in order to save costs on real estate and power, or to give employees flexibility. Telecommuting, specifically, can keep employees closer to their families and help them avoid long commutes. Employees spend less time in traffic but, in exchange, spend large portions of the day on e-mail, teleconferences, or even web conferences. They have fewer opportunities for face-to-face communication like chats in the hallway, company cafeteria, or coffee room. Consequently, telecommuters may feel detached and no longer a part of the larger company and the company's mission.

The Next Move Is Yours

The problems of information sharing in an organization are certainly familiar to you. Undoubtedly, you have spent time on a project only to find out that someone else has already solved the same problem you struggled to resolve. You've been frustrated that, once again, your team hasn't had access to the most updated information. Or, in a quest to solve a customer complaint, you've gone down many paths only to find out that the person who could answer your question is "no longer with the company."

You've learned in this chapter that social business software can generate meaningful business value for an organization. Now it's your turn to prove it at your company. Whether you choose to a social platform for your workgroup or for a specific business process, it's time to define your project and plan your rollout. Let's go.

CHAPTER 5

DESIGNING AND EXECUTING A SUCCESSFUL ROLLOUT

THE INTERSECTION OF TECHNOLOGY, BEHAVIOR, AND BUSINESS VALUE

We've talked a lot about technology—mobile, cloud, big data— and, of course, the actual social platform that leverages—and gets leveraged by—all of them. We've also explored how several companies have created business value using a social platform. Technology creates the capabilities that lead to business value, but technology alone won't win the war. The key to a making a social business platform implementation stick is combining all three— technology, business value, and change management (behavior change)—as shown in Figure 5.1.

Specifically, this chapter focuses on how to determine your starting point, choose a platform, launch a social business solution, run a change management process, and measure your progress.

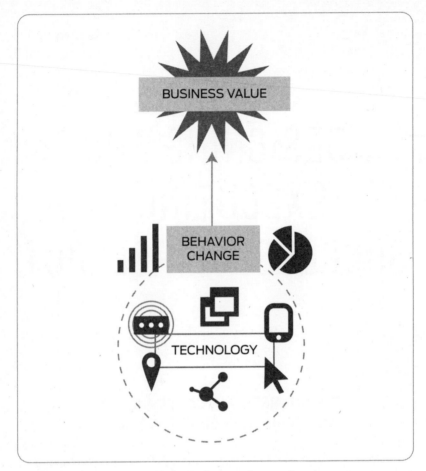

FIGURE 5.1. The Social Business Success Equation

Assess

Start with a Defined Use Case

When you introduce a social business platform, you are likely to see benefits in at least one of four areas: hard dollar savings, improved outcomes (i.e., higher win rate), accelerated outcomes (i.e., time to close deal), or productivity gains. Your team/department/company will value each of these outcomes differently at different times. Let whatever outcome your team values most determine where you start. Then, choose a project that will enable you to capture benefits in one of these areas.

In the previous chapter we focused mainly on business value implementations and de-emphasized the aspirational, wall-to-wall projects. This was intentional. Your best chance for success with a social business platform is to start with a defined use case. Some popular use cases are employee onboarding, sales enablement, customer service, and marketing campaign/event management.

Build a Business Case

Once you've decided on your first implementation, you need to build a business case. The business case justifies why you are embarking on the particular project you've selected. It asks, "Why change and why now?"

A lot of companies skip this step because they don't know how to do it. Don't follow their lead!

You need to be able to present a business case that will move your enterprise to a better place. This place is one where you are not just working harder, but you are reaching those outcomes that are important to your business in terms of top line and bottom line metrics.

When you start with a specific use case, you can be clear on the benefits that you expect from the platform. With a wall-to-wall implementation, it's very hard to know what the technology's impact will be over time. Without that insight, it's a challenge to give people a real reason to learn how to use the platform and, eventually, adopt it.

The challenge here is to prove that the platform will have an impact on a specific process. The benefit of focus is that you can be very clear of what you will do on the social business platform. Even before you put it in team members' hands, you must offer them a business value assessment or estimate of quantifiable effect that the platform will have on a certain process or function.

Here is your game plan:

First, establish benchmarks both for your industry and for your company.

Then project the value that you expect the platform will create.[1]

Consider a sales enablement implementation in a sales organization of a large consulting firm. You predict that enabling the sales team with the right information and tools will increase the win rate and reduce cost of sales. Below is an illustration of how the firm saved $1.7 million when it introduced a social platform for sales enablement. First leaders estimated how the platform would lead to hard dollar savings, productivity gains, improved outcomes, and accelerated outcomes, as shown in Figure 5.2.

When the firm drilled down in hard dollar savings, the company estimated that decreased travel—and that alone!—would lead to a $1.7 million savings. A simple calculation is shown in Figure 5.3.

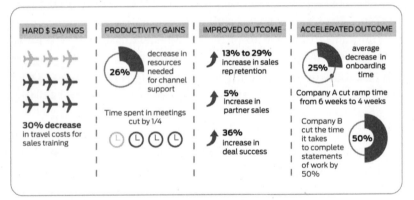

FIGURE 5.2. Sales Enablement Business Value Assessment

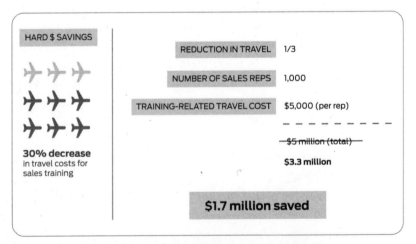

FIGURE 5.3. Sales Enablement Business Value Assessment

While the example above is very high level, the more detailed you can be about the impact you expect to get, the better. Make well-judged assumptions about your business, find benchmarks to compare against, tailor those benchmarks to your business, and, finally, project a number, and show why it is achievable. Figure 5.4 shows ample inputs, outputs, and overall revenue impact of a social business platform for sales enablement.

If, alternatively, you'd started with a wall-to-wall rollout, you have no guarantee that people will use the platform for anything that provides business value. People might just get on and talk to each other. Not that communication is bad, it's just not that valuable to have yet another communication tool. When you roll out the platform to the entire company at once, you have no goal or specific quantitative outcome. You leave a lot to serendipity.

Starting Small and Making Steady Progress

When you start with a discrete use case, you can be clear about what you hope to get as a result. We all want to escape the Red Queen's race; we want to reach that wonderful future where social technology transforms an enterprise. The only way to get there is by adding many successful rollouts—well-understood

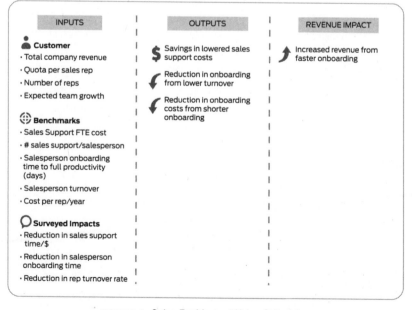

FIGURE 5.4. Sales Enablement Value Calculator

use cases—together. When you can point to these examples, you make it make it crystal clear that the social business platform is working. Intention and behavior change is everything.

Just throwing social platform on your business and commanding it to change won't work. It's like the Red Queen telling Alice to, "Run faster."

These individual use cases are like individuals or even states in a grassroots movement. U.S. Supreme Court Justice Louis D. Brandeis once commented that this bottoms-up adoption also works in the United States:

> It is one of the happy incidents of the federal system that a single courageous state may, if its citizens choose, serve as a laboratory; and try novel social and economic experiments without risk to the rest of the country.[2]

Similarly, departments in a larger corporation can implement a social platform on a small scale first before taking on a risky roll-out that involves the entire organization. Each functional use case you initiate in your enterprise is like a load-bearing pillar. Each pillar represents a clear articulation of why the team is using it. Each pillar is also a small win in the journey toward a wall-to-wall connected company. But it is an experiment nonetheless. The more pillars you erect, the more ways you change the way people work in your organization, the stronger your organization becomes, and the more connected your employees are to the technology.

Once you have several pillars firmly grounded—several business or function specific implementations in place—the final stages of connecting everyone in the organization happens fast.

Beware of False Value

You can't build a business case for a social business platform with soft value. Many projects lead with the value of social as driving feelings of connectedness, giving people visibility into work happening in other departments, and locating information faster. You might hear stats like, "68 percent of users say that social simplifies the process of communicating with colleagues in different locations or departments," or "79 percent are more exposed to new ideas and innovations in their organization."

All well and good. Connectivity and transparency are, no doubt, valuable to an organization. They just aren't sufficiently valuable as starting points. When you go in selling the value of collaboration to an executive committee, you're failing to point to the things they care about most. It's not that they're against collaboration. But collaboration, on its own, is not a compelling value proposition to motivate behavior change and make an investment.

Executives focus on outcomes: revenue, cost reductions, and, of course, profit. When you make a business case for a social business platform with soft value, you aren't focusing on the things that are most important to executives.

Pick the Right Platform

You'll hear the technology won't determine success of a project. True, but it still matters which technology you pick. When you evaluate a platform, make sure you ask the vendor the following questions:

Is the platform purpose built for my use case? For instance, if you are going to use a product for sales enablement, you need to ask yourself if it is going to work out of the box for that purpose or if it's a very generic platform.

Does it integrate easily into my ecosystem and adjust to the future? You need to look at all the systems that your company uses today and all of the systems that a social platform will touch. The social platform will need to be flexible enough to respond to an uncertain future in the way you need.

Many companies believe they can buy one software suite and get all the applications they need. They assume a single vendor will address every issue and that all the vendors' applications will work well together. If your business is large enough, this vision is, unfortunately, a pipe dream. Even if you did try to limit your technology to one vendor, you wouldn't be able to get your IT landscape to this state for a long time. Instead, make interoperability your focus. Pick a platform that will work well with what you have today.

It's also important not to confuse the tools you actually use with other technologies that offer similar capabilities. For instance, if you have a tool that provides sales force automation but you heavily rely on another tool for relationship management, make sure that your platform works with the relationship management tool you use.

Can my workers use it? You want users to be able to get on the platform easily—and then want to use it. It should be as intuitive as that. Though usability of enterprise tools hasn't been an issue in the past, now that employees have intuitive tools in their personal lives, they have higher expectations for the technology they use at work. Few people read an instruction manual for an iPhone!

Do the analytics show real business value? Typically, a social business platform will offer four main types of analytics:

▸ Community analytics: Community health, level of engagement
▸ Business metrics: Time to close a deal, time to answer customer's request
▸ Social graph-driven analytics: Number of recommendations, number of documents uploaded, number of "likes"
▸ Business intelligence: Information on why a key performance indicator is trending down

You could imagine this data on a matrix, as shown in Figure 5.5.

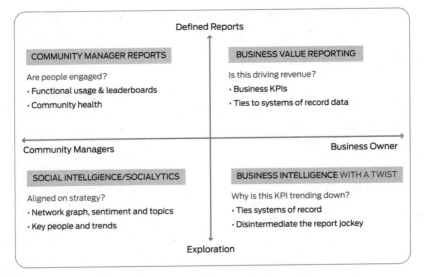

FIGURE 5.5. Social Business Platform Analytics: Reporting, Analytics, and Insights

These analytics vary in their usefulness. Generally, community analytics are overdone. If you think about community analytics like vital statistics in a hospital, community analytics tell us the patient has a pulse but few details beyond that. How is the liver functioning? What is the oxygen level? If a system can only show how many people are logging on to a system, that's not enough.

Business intelligence is usually too heavy handed. It's not clear what to do with the information.

Business metrics, however, reflect things that you built your business case on, such as time to sign a deal, time to resolve a customer complaint, time to launch a campaign, etc. Social graph analytics help you gauge sentiment and see how people are connecting on certain topics. Both of these sets of metrics are useful.

Is it enterprise ready? The solution needs to scale, provide security, and support compliance and localization. These attributes are important if you want to get the IT department's approval as they enable IT to protect the business.

Does the vendor have industry proven leadership? Make sure that the company has worked with many customers—you don't want to be its guinea pig. When you look at references, the list should include companies you've heard of and that are willing to talk to you frankly.

What's the product road map? The road map is the company's vision for its technology. It maps how companies will use the product over time. It shouldn't be just a backlog of features. The product road map should match your company's vision for where things are headed. If you are moving toward security based on identity management, for instance, you don't want to choose a product that relies on a different method.

PLAN: UNDERSTAND THE FROM>TO

Overcoming Resistance with Technology That Provides Immediate Value

While social technology is easy for users to learn, it challenges people to work differently. They will have to move from one way of working to a new way.

This movement requires people to change. Change is always hard. It will be resisted. For one, users have little willingness to try a new technology. The average worker has seen many tools come and go in the enterprise. Even if the existing environment is dysfunctional, employees aren't clear whether new tools make their lives easier or more complicated.

Enterprise workers are exhausted. Many still remember the change management processes associated with wall-to-wall enterprise resource planning (ERP) implementations. Then, consultants rolled out a technology to the entire company simultaneously. Consultants went task-by-task, process-by-process, teaching individuals how to complete their work on a new system. If someone was working in accounts payable, for instance, change management consultants showed her how to work on the ERP's general ledger rather than entering data on a spreadsheet. Hundreds of consultants worked with every team in an organization to lead this process change.

ERP and other big system rollouts, however, shared many shortcomings. The extensive projects were very difficult to manage and complete successfully; transformation touched almost every part of a business. And, because massive change is hard for an organization to swallow, these sprawling projects had a high risk of failure. When you introduce a social business platform, you focus on behavior change for a specific use case—the part that matters to an individual or team—so users exploit the technology to get what they want. This improves focus and, most importantly, likelihood of success.

Learn How to Change Habits

When you introduce a social business platform, you will be changing habits. In Charles Duhigg's bestselling book *The Power of Habit: Why We Do What We Do in Life and Business*, the author explains that habits emerge in order to help the brain save effort. According to Duhigg, habits include a three-step loop:

First, there is a cue, a trigger that tells your brain to go into automatic mode and which habit to use. Then there is the routine, which can be physical or mental or emotional. Finally, there is the reward, which helps your brain figure out if this particular loop is worth remembering for the future.

When a habit emerges, the brain stops fully participating in decision making. It stops working so hard, or diverts focus to other tasks. So unless you deliberately fight a habit—unless you find new routines—the pattern will unfold automatically.

Habits can be changed. Starbucks taught its baristas to handle "moments of adversity"—an angry customer complaining that the coffee was too cold or they got the wrong drink—by teaching them a routine that helped them establish new habits. Instead of getting scared or angry, Starbucks proposed a plan for dealing with unhappy customers and attached a memorable mnemonic device, LATTE, to the plan. The LATTE method involves listening to the customer, acknowledging the complaint, taking action by solving the problem, thanking them, and then explaining why the problem occurred. When people can decide ahead of time how they will react to a cue—in this case, an angry customer—they can change the way they react and develop new behavior habits.[3]

Launch a Focused Changed Process

As difficult as it is to change, it's unavoidable. The best way to approach changing processes is to make two process maps: the process today and the process in the future. You need to assess where today's tools—instant messenger, e-mail, sales force automation—aren't working. To make any implementation successful, a company must change its communication habits.

Imagine you run account management at an engineering firm. You spend a lot of your time completing statements of work (SOWs) for prospective customers. You use e-mail to coordinate and communicate with engineering, design and development, service, legal, and administration. You take the SOW, break it into pieces, and then send it out to the people you believe will best complete the various sections. As the account manager, you serve as the hub of knowledge and determine who receives which e-mails about the SOW.

We've talked about the problems with this process: it's inefficient, slow, and fails to include all relevant participants and knowledge. The information comes from people whom you, the account manager, know. No one in the process can see the content that others contribute or notice contradictions. Even you, the account manager, can't read the e-mails between contributors or the discussions that led to the finished SOW.

Does this process produce the best SOW? Unlikely.

Let's say you introduce a social business platform to your team with two goals: shorten the time it takes to complete a SOW and increase the win rate.

In training, you, the account manager, start the process by posting the SOW on the platform. Everyone who would normally be involved in developing logs on to the platform learns how to post comments, edit a document, upload reference documents, and even initiate a poll. They see conversations around different topics—pricing, planning, logistics—and contribute their ideas. Then, when the process is complete, someone in the group reviews the proposal. The process of delivering an SOW on the platform should take less time and receive more oversight from a larger group.

Beyond just being a less cumbersome tool, the platform offers other benefits. As team members use the platform, they build up a knowledge base. Everything that people discuss is visible. And, instead of the knowledge leaving the company with inevitable turnover, it stays on the platform. When new hires come on board and learn to pitch to a certain industry, they don't just read a manual or do computer-based training in a vacuum. Instead, they get on the platform, locate team members with industry expertise, and find past conversations and commentary. New hires also get complementary information (presentations, pricing models) automatically. Finally, the platform saves a fringe group of domain experts—people that receive multiple inquiries on the same topic—from constantly repeating themselves. These individuals contribute just once to the platform, and then the whole team can access their knowledge.

That's efficiency!

Draw a Process Map

A process map helps ensure a team understands every detail and role in a specific process. The clearer you are about what the change looks like, who is affected, and how each person/team will proceed, the better you can articulate the path forward. Figures 5.6 and 5.7 illustrate the "before" and "after" for a company's marketing campaign management process. Like Starbucks' LATTE method, it outlines how people complete a process without social technology and then how they will do the same process on a social platform.

PAIN POINT	BEFORE SOCIAL BUSINESS PLATFORM	AFTER SOCIAL BUSINESS PLATFORM
ALIGNING ON BRIEF	• Creative brief is written by corporate or product marketing, then is e-mailed to various agencies and forwarded around to get feedback.	• Brief is written collaboratively across the company and with agencies to gain alignment. • As people/agencies come on and off the project, they can see the final brief and the conversations around them.
GETTING APPROVALS/ SIGN-OFFS	• Sign-offs on brief, content, etc., require meetings, e-mails, conference calls, leading to delays.	• Sign-offs and approvals can be had in-line online much faster.
SHARING AND COLLABORATING ON WORK	• Agencies work independently to develop concepts, e-mail or post docs to a file sharing website.	• Agencies can work together with marketing to develop the concept. • Assets and insights can be shared across agencies (especially needed as people/agencies join and leave the project).
INCLUDING SALES IN CAMPAIGN	• Keeping sales abreast requires additional meetings/presentations. • Difficult to gather commentary/input from sales people while the campaign is running.	• Sales management and frontline employees can quickly understand the breadth of all marketing campaigns and how it affects them. • Sales people can provide real-time input on the impact of the campaign they are seeing.
INTERNAL CROSS-CAMPAIGN COORDINATION	• Different divisional marketing teams are not coordinated, missing synergistic opportunities (e.g. media buying).	• All divisional marketing departments can see what all of the divisions are doing to ensure alignment and cooperation.

FIGURE 5.6. How a Social Business Platform Addresses Marketing Campaign Development Pain Points

PAIN POINT	BEFORE SOCIAL BUSINESS PLATFORM	AFTER SOCIAL BUSINESS PLATFORM
RUNNING TESTS AND GATHERING INSIGHTS	· Results and learnings from tests are not teasy to share across the various groups to ensure appropriate targeting / adjustments.	· Campaign tests across all agencies/functions are collected in one place for real-time discussion and adjustment. · Next actions/changes can be managed in one central place.
MANAGING AND DISTRIBUTING CONTENT	· Digital media/content are spread across numerous servers (and networks), taking time and making version control difficult.	· All digital content is in one central place (or linked to), ensuring that the right version gets to the right place at the right time.
MONITORING IN-MARKET PERFORMANCE	· Campaign updates and data are e-mailed around or spread across intranet sites. · Little or no support of a "conversation" around the data.	· Platform provides a central portal for real-time campaign feedback across all campaigns (including feedback from agencies, marketing, and sales).
CAPTURING LEARNINGS	· Postmortems are oftentimes not conducted, or if they are filed away and not referenced in the future.	· Platform provides a full real-time record of all campaign activity to reference, whether a postmortem is collected or not.

FIGURE 5.7. How a Social Business Platform Addresses Marketing Campaign Development Pain Points (continued)

Case Study: Eloqua, Social Customer Service

Eloqua launched a social platform called Topliners to more effectively—and economically—serve customers. Eloqua, a wholly owned subsidiary of Oracle, develops marketing automation software. The software supports campaign execution, testing, measurement, prospect profiling, and lead management. More than 50,000 marketers use Eloqua—more than every other marketing automation vendor combined. Clients include Adobe, AON, Dow Jones, ADP, Fidelity, Polycom, and National Instruments.

Eloqua customers liked to talk with each other and share experiences. However, with customers around the country and the world, many customers were not able to attend Eloqua events. According to Heather Foeh, director of customer culture, customers were anxious to solve their own problems: "We started our Topliners community because we really heard from our customers that they were looking for a place to interact with each other and self-support."

Eloqua wanted to position itself as a thought leader in the area of digital marketing and drive its customers' success, two levers that would also increase sales. With these outcomes in mind, Eloqua built in functionality for customer collaboration and customer self-service for customers around the world.

In the planning phase of its project, Eloqua discovered that it would have three types of users in the community: executives, operational marketers, and tactical marketers. The executives, chief marketing officers (CMOs), set the marketing strategy for the company. They were interested in learning about visionary marketers and industry trends. The community needed to have enough content to keep the CMOs coming back to the community. Marketing managers fell into the operational category; they would use the customer community to gather peers' success stories and perform benchmarking. Finally, one group of users had a very tactical agenda. They wanted help fixing problems and implementing programs.

Since Eloqua would serve three types of customers, it needed to understand each group's different requirements. Eloqua took a position of, "We are here to host a conversation that will help you—the

CMO, marketing manager, or marketing coordinator—achieve your objectives." By focusing on what members wanted, Eloqua could prioritize what features to build in first and spur adoption.

Once Eloqua defined user requirements, it could ask the right questions to determine if the company had the resources it needed to give each audience the appropriate content. The questions the company asked included the following:

▶ Are we dealing with a group of people that will volunteer that information?
▶ Do we have resources that will sustain this as a program? If not, do we need to build to meet this need? Do we need to hire guest bloggers, recruit them?

In the planning process, Eloqua learned that it couldn't create a community and expect users to contribute. Instead, internally planners discussed how to launch programs that would encourage users to talk and make the community self-sustaining. Like a well-built fire, Eloqua needed to select its kindling wisely. Once the fire started, it would burn how it burned, but the more deliberately Eloqua planned the initial programs it launched on the community, the greater its success.

The intense focus on customer needs and segments paid off. By 2013, Topliners had over 7,000 members self-servicing their accounts and working with counterparts at other firms. Engagement on Topliners increased renewal and retention rates.

Specifically, 85 percent of customers that renewed their software license with Eloqua were members of Topliners. Of those customers who didn't renew, only 28 percent were members. According to Foeh, Topliners became part of doing business at Eloqua:

> Every month, salespeople say they closed a deal because a customer says they saw something on Topliners. This group has contributed to topline revenue growth. It's revolutionized our business; it has become part of our DNA and part of our culture.

PLAN: SET UP FOR SUCCESS

Once you've planned the assessment stage, it's time to look at integrations, content, and training. You want the platform to be working with your other systems and have relevant content when the first users log on.

Integrate the Platform into Your Existing Environment

You'll need to integrate social business software with your company's existing IT systems. It will need to connect to content management tools, communication software, and systems of record. But integrating social with every enterprise application is too time consuming and expensive. Instead, the people who will actually be using the product—not IT—should revisit the business problem they are trying to solve and, from there, determine the integrations they need. Here are a few sample approaches:

Customer Service

If a company is implementing social customer service, the enterprise should integrate the software with the case management system (trouble ticketing), customer service/product knowledge base, and a system that tracks customer issues.

Sales

If social business software is directed at the sales organization, integrate it with sales force automation software. Similarly, a social platform for product marketing should integrate with marketing automation software.

Content Management

A social intranet project should connect to an existing content management system, SharePoint (if applicable), LDAP,[4] e-mail, and Microsoft Office.

Cartridges, out-of-the-box connectors, can eliminate the need for integrations with many popular applications. For instance, if a company is running specific web apps like Salesforce.com, MS Dynamics, Office 365, SAP, Netsuite, Google Docs, and

LinkedIn, a cartridge can connect the social software platform and specific web applications. Then, when a user is looking at the record in Salesforce.com, or a document in Google Docs, the social software's reading pane will show relevant content and conversations related to that specific record or app.

Seed Content

A social business platform has to have content so that the first time people visit, the system looks legitimate even if it's the most initial phase of a rollout. No one likes to go to a party and be the only guest!

Beyond seeding the platform with content, the project manager or group facilitator can simulate the response of a system and take a role of "fakin' it until you're makin' it." For instance, when a salesperson from one region asks a marketing question on the social tool, the community manager alerts the product managers to the question and directs them to post their answers on the social platform. Until reps start seeing timely answers to their posts, the community manager must remind product managers to log on to the system. As activity on the platform gains momentum, the facilitator features valuable content, then tags it to make sure the right users see it.

If a company is deliberate about these processes for long enough (approximately three months), the group reaches homeostasis where sales reps find that they can ask questions and get answers faster using social business software than by using e-mail or phone.

Similarly, in external customer social platforms, the community manager shouldn't wait for customers to start collaborating on the community site. Instead, prior to the launch, the manager would recruit champions from the customer community who will share tips about a certain product. When a customer posts a question, the community manager e-mails one of the designated customers who then answers. Eventually, these customer champions log on and answer questions without prompting.

Train the Users

It is one thing to tell people to change—but they must have the skills to change. The fallacy with social business is that it should be so easy that it needs no training. A well-designed social platform is easy to use, but not everyone knows how to collaborate effectively and apply the principles of social business to get work done.

Training requirements vary by company. Some users need an outline that gives them the general steps they should take when they start to use the system. Others need explicit, paint by number–type guidance. Your company should focus on best practices in using social software to solve problems.

One important step is training advocates. Subsequently, you need to encourage them to go out to their networks and recruit others. Advocates should demonstrate to their colleagues that introducing social business software is an exciting thing for the company and, prior to the rollout, generate content that the company needs.

Once the platform is live, a great advocate will ask people to talk about specific topics, ask questions of the community, answer questions, push other users to give opinions, and share their experiences on blogs.

—————— IMPLEMENT ——————

Burn the Ships

One of the most important things you'll do in this phase is burn the ships; you need to turn off other tools so that teams and individuals turn to the social platform rather than the tools it is trying to replace. These include intranets, portals, and document management systems.

Offer Incentives/Motivation

In designing incentives, you should first focus on what's in it for the end user. Often the most powerful motivators and the most sustainable programs involve tapping into individuals' intrinsic motivations. A good incentive program will leverage the research of Daniel Pink and provide opportunities for autonomy, mastery, and purpose—as well as traditional recognition.[5]

Using carrots and sticks in combination works best. For instance, in trying to encourage a sales representative to use the platform, an internal social business software advocate must make the case that if reps change their behavior, they will get answers to their questions and close deals faster. This is the carrot. Or, when a sales rep uses e-mail to elicit the team's knowledge on a specific customer, sales leadership can repetitively push the user to the social platform instead. This is the stick. Make use of both!

Gamification

Recognition—either from managers or peers—is, hands down, the biggest motivator to encourage employees to use social business software. Gamification, a methodology developed by Bunchball, involves applying the data-driven motivational techniques from video games to non-game experiences. It takes techniques that game designers have employed for years—leveling up, leaderboards, badges, competition, transparency, etc.—and uses them to motivate people to do more high-value activities. Using gamification, social community managers can give their users goals that encourage participation or drive specific behaviors. When users reach certain levels or complete a goal, they earn specific status and recognition.

Participation, especially in the beginning of a social business software project, can be difficult to muster when users don't know what's in it for them. Some users will share information without any encouragement. Others need some prodding. Gamification drives participation because it uses motivators based off fundamental human needs and desires—reward, status, achievement, self-expression, competition, and altruism, as shown in Figure 5.8.

As users live their lives online and generate activity data, companies accumulate vast amounts of information they can then use to drive users to higher-value activities, reward behavior, and spur competition. Until now, however, this activity data has remained in silos or in one-off programs such as frequent flyer programs.

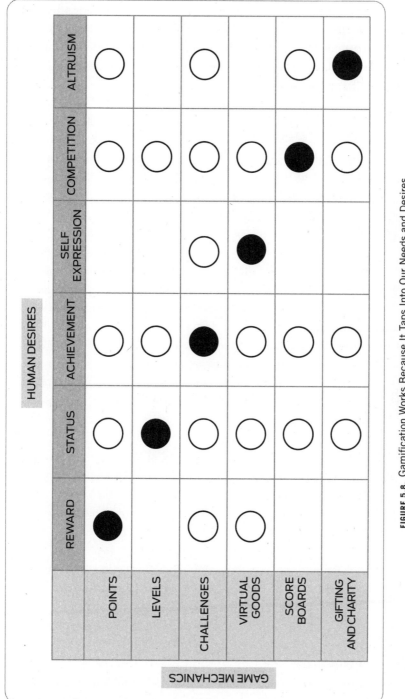

FIGURE 5.8. Gamification Works Because It Taps Into Our Needs and Desires
Source: Rajat Paharia, CEO Bunchball

The convergence of mobility, cloud, and big data opens up new opportunities for gamification. Rajat Paharia, founder and chief product officer of Bunchball, envisions a flexible platform that can take user activity data and use it to motivate users and drive what he refers to as Loyalty 3.0.[6]

Case Study: SolarWinds

SolarWinds is a company that uses gamification and badges to drive certain user behavior. Founded in 1999, SolarWinds is a public company that sells IT management and monitoring software to over 100,000 customers worldwide from Global 1,000 enterprises to small businesses.

SolarWinds launched thwack, a customer community, to enable customers to collaborate with other customers, SolarWinds employees, and technology partners. Members can also take part in discussions, watch video tutorials, contact support, download tools, and read blogs.

SolarWinds wanted to drive engagement in certain activities and get users to connect with sales and customer service agents. Gamification enabled the company to increase the interaction in particular forums and collect specific information. Outcomes included the following:

▶ Increase in the number of customer stories about product usage
▶ Increase in the number of views and usage of the platform's discussion capabilities
▶ Collection of information on new product ideas and feature requests

As users adopted the tool, the community team used the platform to help monitor users' activity and solidify the reputation of top users and advocates, labeling them as MVPs.

Product Rewards

One way to reward contributors is to give individuals advance access to products. For instance, a company can give the highest-rated contributors/product advocates the opportunity to try out a product in a test environment and be the first users to give feedback on a new product. Companies can also reward community advocates with mobile devices or even upgrades at user conferences. Great incentives can help advocates evangelize the value of the community. For instance, Pearson gave Flip video cameras to the community advocates. These individuals visited different departments in the company and spotlighted success stories.

Beyond material rewards, a company can offer community members early or exclusive access to content, extra power or moderating rights on a community, or introductions to company executives.

Provide Support When Needed

Prior to the implementation, an enterprise will need to know how to form a team, how much time everyone will need to dedicate to the project, and the terms of their involvement.

Once the platform is in regular use, the enterprise must have a plan as to who will support users when they are interacting with the platform.

Measure and Communicate Success

Measurement is part of management. Companies must keep tabs on the community's health. They need to ask themselves if employees or customers are using the system, if they using it for the intended purposes, and if it is providing the specific value it was set up to offer.

Once individuals and teams start using the platform, the business owner should cull success stories from participants and disseminate these through the organization.

BEST PRACTICES FOR ENTERPRISE-WIDE IMPLEMENTATIONS

While the suggestions above apply to any implementation, if your organization is intent on a wall-to-wall implementation from the get-go, the best practices of top-down change management still apply. First, you'll need to gain executive sponsorship;

it will be nearly impossible to be successful without their support. Next, you need to invest in communications and make a big bang leading up to and following the rollout. You need to make it clear to everyone what you are doing, who will do what, and change the behavior of hundreds—if not hundreds of thousands—of people at once. You'll need to integrate every system that users might need to work with the social platform and maintain visibility to compliance. Once people start using the platform, you'll need to celebrate wins and successes across the organization.

Does this sound like an ERP rollout from the 1990s? It's not a coincidence. It's a giant massive change management exercise.

Identify Stakeholders

Who are the stakeholders? As the team rolls out a social platform, the stakeholders will identify themselves. They include everyone who will use or be affected by the platform. Common stakeholders include the executive team, managers, enablement teams, key subject-matter experts, role models, casual participants, heavy participants, general employees, and even, perhaps, customers.

Subsequently, the team should conduct stakeholder analysis to understand each stakeholder's issues and generate ways to address these issues.

Consider Cultural Biases

Organizations must consider how the solution will connect to the culture. Not every company is at the same starting point or readiness point for a social business platform. Evaluating cultural readiness involves understanding both top management and prospective users at all levels of the organization.

Cultural Readiness at a Global Bank

John Stepper, a managing director focused on collaboration and social media tools at a global bank, was part of a team that evaluated social business software for the bank. In the process of meeting with different software vendors, prospective users and the IT professionals asked questions about data infrastructure, metadata, tagging data, and other technical questions. What Stepper felt the team should have focused on, however, was cultural fit of a social platform at an investment bank:

> Banks, particularly investment banks, are competitive places. People don't share information readily or naturally because they may be competing with other departments in the firm. We've been trained not to write things down; writing things down can make your life more complicated. Once you write things down, more rules apply. Instead, people try to limit communication to people they know and trust.[7]

It was clear that if the social business platform was going to have any impact on the business, the culture needed to change. Bank employees needed to share their activities and processes in a way that was visible to others at the firm. A social business platform could simplify information exchange, but the company wouldn't get any major benefit from the software without a profound cultural shift.

What worked at the bank was demonstrating the benefits of the platform first within a community of practice—groups of people doing the same job. It was a way of starting small and felt less risky to the group. Stepper explained to this community, "Let's start first with your own group." The communities were safe places to share information. Once users got comfortable sharing within their own community, moving outside the community was a lot easier. As Stepper recalled:

> Individuals realized that if they participated in community, everyone who saw what they could do could learn from them. In turn, the individuals gained visibility. Developing a higher profile helped them access people, get a new position, and shape their reputation inside a big company.

The competitive nature of the bank's work environment and external forces didn't seem to be conducive to social collaboration—yet the social business platform gained traction at the bank. Individuals contributed expertise and answered questions because the chance to gain recognition from peers and access new opportunities trumped their cultural challenges. Eventually, they felt more comfortable sharing outside of the immediate group—and the social platform became ubiquitous.

Design a Launch That Assumes Longevity

When you introduce a new technology, you are asking people to support something that, in some cases, they don't think they need. To get everyone in the company—4,000 or even 400,000 people—on one wall-to-wall social business platform is a challenge.

Many companies, mistakenly, approach the wall-to-wall implementation with either a pilot or time-boxed trial. Best to avoid these methods! They are actually one reason that wall-to-wall projects can be risky.

Pilot/Soft Launch

A manufacturing organization was ready to purchase the software, when an executive spoke up, "I'm sold on social business software, I see how it has been successful in other companies—but how do we know my people are going to use it?"

One way to get users to quickly adopt, especially when users and executive are skeptical, is to do a soft launch or a small, contained project. When a company has a low risk tolerance, the chance to "screw up small" can spur a company to try a social business platform. An implementation for an IT department, for instance, can work well as a soft launch.

Now, the bad news. Though a soft launch can be easy and low friction, when a company does a soft launch it may indicate a lack of commitment and confusion. When you begin a project without the end in mind, it is unlikely you will find value.

Timebox Trial

Another method to encourage adoption in a launch is to "timebox" a trial. A project's sponsor can say, "We are going to try this tool for the next three weeks. It will reduce the number of one-off questions you answer and reduce the number of questions that reach you, period. Are you willing to try it for three weeks?" It's difficult for users to reject something when they know that the time they must spend is limited.

A timebox trial can work well as a way to get a project moving and spread awareness. However, everyone involved in the project is driving toward time, not toward an outcome. It's hard to keep everyone focused on a goal if they don't know what that goal is.

Waves

While people like to start with a pilot or timebox trial, we think these methods increase the risk of failure. Instead, adding successive groups of users is a great way to introduce social software. A global tax and consulting firm once took this approach to its social intranet rollout when it launched "waves" (see case study in Chapter 4).

The firm's employees had lived through many rollouts and, according to one manager, were "tired of pilots." Rolling out the social platform—Spark—in waves lasting 90 days created excitement around the initiative and presented the new communication platform as something other than "one more pilot." Employees understood that the company was serious about social enterprise software and committed to its success.

Instead of focusing on the most strategic groups for the first wave, the firm targeted groups where the most senior partner was excited and could see potential in the tool. It needed people who, according to one executive, "wouldn't fall at the first hurdle." This process allowed the firm to lock in one group and make sure they were on board before adding another group of users.

The firm's team chose just 12 groups to be part of the first wave. The firm gave these first wave workgroups white-glove treatment, including all of the consulting, resources, and guidance they needed as they rolled out social business software. Many of these groups were very vocal about their positive experience and spread their excitement to other teams. The groups that used the social platform first became an exclusive group. The firm also let each country determine how it wanted to roll out Spark. For instance, Singapore performed a flash mob–type song and dance to introduce Spark.

Use Compelling Communications

Communication is easily the most popular change technique, but it's usually overemphasized. People don't change purely because they receive new information; every doctor who's ever told a patient to start exercising knows this is true!

Instead, enterprises should view communication as a way to build excitement about change. Many of the most successful social business software projects started with a great amateur video describing the new platform. Beyond generating buzz, communication should focus on making sure everyone is informed, at every stage of the process, with the right information at the right time. Communications should reduce anxiety, overcome inertia, build excitement, and offer a uniform message about the platform.

Once individuals and teams start using the platform, the project leader should cull success stories from participants and disseminate these throughout the organization.

Identify Role Models

After the platform is live, an individual or group in the company needs to be responsible for ongoing management. Role models' involvement can highly correlate to success. These role models include the following:

Executives

Critical participants, especially those who will be directly affected by the change. The companies that deliver business value from social business software share at least one commonality: C-level sponsorship.

Social Platform Champion

Well-connected politically, respected by decision makers, and able to get stuff done. He or she is usually at the level of a senior director. Without this driver, the project will plateau.

In terms of commitment, if the project is more strategic, the individual person will be 100 percent dedicated to the project. When it is more tactical, it could be just a third of that person's job.

Managers

Individuals who influence the behavior of their teams. The best way to engage these mid-level managers—people such as product marketing and sales managers—is to first identify their concerns. Gathering this information will ensure that a rollout can happen smoothly so that the company can quickly become better, faster, and stronger.

Advocates

Avid supporters who help their networks support the change. These are the employees who, in a meeting, will say, "Let's use our social network to come up with new ideas and solve the problem."

Vocal pockets of users that love that platform are extremely helpful in weathering any storms that may occur. For instance, when some users have difficulties accessing their data, a strong group of users praising the platform can make these unhappy users' complaints less noticeable.

Subject-Matter Experts

They buy in to the new way of working and understand how they benefit from the tool. They'll need to invest time in seeding content when the project starts, but once their knowledge is available to a wider audience they'll get fewer requests for information.

The company should also assign roles and responsibilities for governance and discuss how it will handle specific kinds of behavior. The company might need policies that can address inappropriate user behavior—such as rude or derogatory comments, or even humor that is lost (or, worse, inappropriate) in translation. The company should also discuss human resources and legal policies.

If the social platform will mainly focus on external users, organizations should follow a similar process and find passionate customers who can act as advocates. These individuals know the product inside and outside and enjoy answering other customers' questions. They might be so enthusiastic as to even reduce the workload for the paid help desk employees. These customers are not necessarily subject matter experts but can get very excited about specific topics.

Figures 5.9 and 5.10 provide more information on the project roles companies have implemented.

REQUIRED PROJECT ROLES

ROLE	COMMON ACTIVITIES
SPONSOR	Reviews, approves strategy. Provides direction and resources to the project team. Promotes value proposition to executive network and general employee population. While not involved in day-to-day activities, a sponsor's participation in the community sends a strong message that the project is important to the business.
BUSINESS OWNER	Has overall responsibility for the social business / community program strategy, governance, policies, leadership, and organization transformation to support a new way of working in the enterprise. Responsible for executive and community communications, measurement dashboards, adoption strategy, code of conduct/acceptable use and other key policies, branding, moderation, customizations, content strategy, and implementation. Benchmarks and implements peer and industry best practices to grow the community and drive business change in all facets of a business' ecosystem (internal, external). Typically a senior level role who is recognized as the program owner and can navigate the enterprise's political and cultural landscape with ease.
ENTERPRISE COMMUNITY MANAGER	Works closely with (and often reporting to) the business owner, often thought of as the "face of the community." Manages day-to-day activity, including training, answering member questions, dealing with inappropriate behavior or abuse, and more. Leads and grows the overall community. Oversees global Working Group activities and "go-to" person for onboarding new communities. Builds and leads SME and Advocate engagement programs to drive member engagement. Creates and analyzes measurement scorecards.
USE CASE OWNERS	Responsible for the successful implementation of a specific use case (for example: Internal Communications, Sales Enablement, IT-based Communities of Practice). This role is especially essential at launch and helping to establish business practices and metrics that will deliver value to users and the business.
PLATFROM OWNER (TECHNICAL)	Has overall responsibility for the platform's release management, architecture, performance, scalability, security, and system health. Interacts with Support and / or Professional Services on technical needs. Oversees development, architectural design, hosting resources and decisions.

FIGURE 5.9. Required Project Roles

BUSINESS USER ROLES

ROLE	COMMON ACTIVITIES
ADVOCATES	Strategic planning business partners who agree to volunteer and get involved in your social business / community program to build groundswell awareness and business use of the platform. They do real work in the community by seeding/leading topics, spreading word of mouth about how to get real work done and can welcome members or provide end user support. Think of advocates as individuals who set the tone for and model best practices in using and engaging in a community.
SMES	Individuals with deep functional/topic knowledge who play a formal, designated role in the community in a way that complements and extends their primary job function in their area of expertise. They provide high-value content, answer questions directly, mentor and guide community members. Role may be optional for internal communities based on topic area, but critical for external communities.

LAUNCH/NEW RELEASE ROLES

ROLE	COMMON ACTIVITIES
TOPIC COMMUNITY MANAGERS	Responsible for the launch, management, member engagement, programming and growth of a specific / topic community.
PROJECT MANAGER	Responsible for managing the launch release. This person will work with their project management counterpart to keep things on track while overseeing the effort of the company's working group to deliver results on time and on budget.
COMMUNI-CATIONS/ MARKETING	Has responsibility to plan, develop, and release communications to support and drive the adoption strategy. Typically an employee communications role for internal communities or a marketing communications role for customer facing community.
SYSTEM ADMIN	Performs day-to-day admin console updates, operations managing users and permission groups, configuration changes, creating spaces as required by the business and other system-wide settings. Works closely with Technical Platform manager on release planning.
USER SUPPORT	Provides daily end user support / help desk operations for the community. Answers questions about site outages or other access issues, provides assistance in recovering lost passwords.

FIGURE 5.10. Business User and Launch/New Release Roles

CSC: A SOCIAL BUSINESS JOURNEY

Hopefully, we've convinced you that going functional area by functional area is the best way to reach value quickly. Of course, some companies will still choose a wall-to-wall implementation. The rollout will be more complicated and time consuming. But, as CSC demonstrates, it's not impossible.

Background

Computer Science Corporation (CSC), CSC is a $14.8 billion, Fortune 200 consulting, systems integration, and outsourcing company with over 90,000 employees and customers in over 90 countries. CSC counts some of the largest organizations in the world among its customers.

Managing a Global, Distributed Workforce

As a provider of information technology services, CSC tends to have a higher percentage of knowledge workers than most companies. The company grappled with how to locate experts and assets, onboard new hires (and transition employees from major accounts), and mitigate loss of intellectual property through attrition. Time and distance made it difficult for CSC to function as a unified organization. With offices in multiple time zones, consultants couldn't just pick up the phone to contact someone in another office.

Identifying Business Drivers

Claire Flanagan, CSC's project leader, stressed the importance of the business case: "By focusing on the business problems and how they tied to CSC's strategy and the evolving marketplace, the team was able to craft a tight business case that was ultimately well received by our executive sponsors." The CSC enterprise 2.0 project team identified critical business realities they believed a 2.0 solution could address:

- It's difficult to locate experts and assets, a barrier to innovation.
- New hires and employees transitioning from customer accounts don't know where to start to become immediately productive.

- ▶ Gen Y workers and early adopters are expected to use tools that are readily available in the consumer marketplace.
- ▶ CSC risks a loss of intellectual property through attrition as well as through employee use of Web 2.0 tools outside the firewall to conduct business.
- ▶ Internal competency around 2.0 technologies has become increasingly important to CSC's core business; an increasing number of customers are asking consultants about new technologies.

To address these challenges, CSC embraced a strategic initiative called C3: connect, communicate, collaborate. C3's mission was to explore the use of the newest enterprise 2.0 technology to "connect people to people, connect people to content, and connect people to communities."

Solution Requirements

CSC's major requirements, across a number of fronts, were as follows.

Track Record of Innovation

CSC sought out a vendor with a track record of delivering major product innovation. CSC felt that enterprise 2.0 technologies were evolving quickly, and users would expect the platform to keep up with marketplace innovations.

Ability to Bridge Internal and External Communities

CSC wanted to create a social business ecosystem. The chosen platform had to go beyond internal collaboration to bridge customer and partner communities. Explained Flanagan, "As a consulting company, this vision was incredibly important to us as our employees often collaborate in private teams with each other, in private project teams with our customers, or in market-facing instances with many customers."

Excellent User Experience

User experience was a priority. John Glowacki, corporate vice president and chief technology officer, recalled, "We had made technology investments that gave more weight to the back end [rather than user experience] and were not being broadly used. We were determined this time around to have our buy decision driven by user feedback." Likewise, John Chambers, CSC senior principal system architect, commented, "We took a people-centric view of the system and focused a lot of energy on making it easy and fun to use right from the start. These efforts paid real dividends with adoption exceeding our most optimistic expectations."

Champions and Advocates

At CSC, the project's driver had the ear of the CEO. To push the implementation, the project driver found 12 volunteers who were bought into the idea of a social intranet. They came from various parts of the organization and around the globe; some were billable, some were not. These individuals loved using social software in their personal lives.

The 12 champions took ownership over the project and trained their colleagues, planned the rollout process, and helped onboard local functional teams and regional users. The champions also seeded content on the platform and built up a cache of use cases. One champion explained how the software enabled the team to create a bid faster, request assistance, accelerate onboarding, and develop new skills.

To encourage natural behavior and reinforce the system's flexibility, the team did not prescribe how CSC employees should engage with each other on the platform or make the platform reflect the company's organization chart. "We decided to let collaboration patterns emerge on their own," said Flanagan, "by allowing users to create groups in a self-service manner for the communities of practice, interests, or projects they needed."

Champions Recruit Advocates

The 12 CSC champions recruited more than 100 advocates who then helped formulate adoption plans, seed content, and test over 200 groups prior to the platform's launch. Gary Lungarini, a business architect at CSC, explained the importance of seeding the tool with content:

> We started with a groundswell of advocates that really got
> things going. They populated the environment and so that

when we went live in our pilot phase, there was already a lot of good content in there. We were able to bring in a lot more people just because they came looking for the content and ways to collaborate, not because we told them to go there. The adoption curve was really phenomenal. It went up really quickly.

When CSC eventually launched the platform in May 2009, the global advocate community answered questions quickly. This, according to Flanagan, was very useful: "As employees got their questions addressed, they became addicted, and then they themselves turned into another powerful wave of advocates helping nurture new users."

Communication and Internal Marketing

CSC marketed the platform as a fulfillment of the C3 strategic initiative: connect, communicate, and collaborate.

- ▶ Connect: Time zones and distance would no longer be barriers. Instead, CSC encouraged employees to use profiles and connections to expand their CSC network.
- ▶ Communicate: The team showed users how to use personal and group blogs to share knowledge or group news.
- ▶ Collaborate: CSC encouraged employees to join groups, collaborate on documents, join discussions, and ask and answer questions.

A Unique, Enterprise-wide Rollout

Rather than launching to a specific team, in May 2009, CSC rolled out its C3 initiative to all 90,000 employees simultaneously. This approach was risky, but CSC worried more about limiting the potential of the project than failing.

CSC believed that the advantage of piloting C3 with people throughout the organization rather than in a single functional area was that the firm could take advantage of global knowledge and expertise. For instance, when a person asked a question, answers could come from experts from around the world, not just those in the user's immediate community.

Second, even though CSC launched a pilot, according to Flanagan, the approach was anything but experimental:

> When we launched the pilot, we went all in. We planned the
> project as if it were a real implementation rather than a pilot. We
> established a champions program, defined multiple initial use
> cases, engaged advocates, and used the best practices of change
> management. Top down, we offered a business case; bottoms
> up we created a groundswell about the platform. We promoted
> longevity by constantly telling our users that the platform
> wouldn't go away if they used it and got business value from it.

C3 was also a major departure from the usual deployment model for internal systems: CSC purchased a cloud-based application rather than an on-premise product. According to John Chambers, "This choice enabled CSC to focus on business and adoption planning and rapidly advance from conceptual phases, to production pilot, and finally to full production in a fraction of the time the traditional deployment model would have required."

One successful adoption practice that proved valuable was offering a "virtual water cooler" for non–work-related topics. As Yvonne Decker, C3 community manager, suggested:

> Sometimes the first post is the hardest to get people to make. By
> offering them a fun place to try out the tool, we made it easy for
> people to get their feet wet and begin thinking about how they
> could use it. The most popular post was "Where is everyone
> from?" which had 3,209 views and 322 posts.

Platform Results Surpass CSC's Highest Expectations

CSC's revenue-generating activities revolve initially around a bid and proposal process. Often, these activities require global team collaboration across different time zones. C3 demonstrated a clear linkage from social business software to the initiative's strategic objectives:

- ▶ Collapsing time and distance barriers to leverage global expertise. A U.S.-based employee posted a request for proposal-related information in C3. This request generated 240 views, 11 global replies, and the right answer from a global colleague in 30 minutes.

► Reducing cycle time for proposal development to reduce customer acquisition costs. Consultants had their questions answered quickly, shaving days off their bid and proposal process.

► Greater ease in locating and engaging internal experts to facilitate collaboration. An employee located the expertise he or she needed for a new business opportunity in two days using C3, a process that previously averaged 5 to 10 days.

► New employee onboarding. Transition teams established buddy and onboarding programs in C3 to help new employees feel immediately connected to the larger whole.

► Collaborating more broadly to drive process efficiencies. Major account teams moved their collaborative efforts to C3, which closed communication gaps around key customer accounts and facilitated timely status and project updates.

CSC has been able to shut down several other applications including portals and intranets, resulting in significant cost savings. According to Lungarini, "Now we have an environment that works better than any of our previous solutions and costs less to run. People have one place to go to do their job; most of our work, globally, happens on C3. Work happens there faster and more efficiently than it did prior to the implementation."

In just 20 weeks, C3 had over 25,000 registered users, 2,100 groups, an average of 1 million page views, and over 150,000 activities per month.

CSC's executives were on board with C3 from the beginning. "Our executive leadership took active roles both in the sponsorship of this program internally and in the communication of this program externally," said Flanagan. It helped that group presidents and other executives led by example. They sent division e-mails to their staff, used the tool to blog, and demonstrated that C3 fit CSC's business.

C3 Expansion

A year after the pilot, the C3 community was powering collaboration throughout the company, and employee adoption had reached 100 percent, with more than 90,000 registered users. "The usage of the C3 platform has been incredible," said Flanagan. "It really is how work gets done at our company."

Later, in 2012, CSC built CSC private community space—Engage Secure™—where 150 customer and partner teams collaborate in a private gated community. This space supports conversations between CSC and trusted third parties in an environment where CSC can protect IP, conversations, and content. As Beth Laking, community manager, explained:

> These project sites enable clients and consultants to share information—everyone can be on the same page. When we work with clients, we are typically delivering a deliverable. When we collaborate on C3, developing the project document and outcomes is an iterative process. Clients can respond to a project in process. The final deliverable they receive is much more robust than they would have received in the past.

The C3 infrastructure has reached over 100,000 employees and subcontractors who participate in over 13,000 groups. Eighty-one percent of employees use C3 on a monthly basis, and over 1 million transactions occur monthly on the system.

No Failures, Only Lessons

When asked to reflect on CSC's social business software journey and how to achieve widespread success, Flanagan shared the following:

> You need to have a good plan, but you also have to be patient and allow the community to adopt and use it for their own purposes. If it is meaningful to them and they find value then the use will grow. There are no failures, only lessons, and if you plan well enough you can inspire the path to get there.

CHAPTER 6

COMMON MISSTEPS IN EMBRACING SOCIAL TECHNOLOGIES

TEMPTATIONS ON THE JOURNEY

The idea that a company could bring in a new technology and achieve measurable business value is a tantalizingly tempting one. Unfortunately, the road is littered with firms that have tried this—and failed. And is that so surprising? Companies face many temptations that lead them off the path to success along their social business journey. Among many potential missteps, a few are so common that it's worth calling them out explicitly.

These are two common mistakes: trying to make old technology feel new or pretending that technology will solve all the business and cultural challenges. It's too easy to confuse a panacea that appears simplistic and approachable with a remedy that will actually get the job done.

So how do you avoid these mundane mistakes? One way is to keep reading. In this chapter, we'll review avoidable errors that have blindsided other enterprises that weren't so vigilant. Go ahead and learn from their mistakes. If you do, it'll be much more likely that you will achieve the business value and the results you want.

BELIEVING SOCIAL TECHNOLOGY
ALONE IS ENOUGH

If you take social features that work really well in the consumer space—@mentioning, blogging, and activity streams—and bring them to a company, you will solve the problem of information management in the enterprise. Right? Wrong! Many of the first companies that rolled out social software were excited about the potential of the technology but fell short on implementation. They thought the system would do everything—it would catch on in their companies like Facebook and mimic the viral nature of LinkedIn. They assumed that people would naturally come together, the right people would interact, they'd address the right problems, and good things would happen. Not so.

Using Adoption and Engagement as Proxies for Success

Many aspects of the tools are reassuringly familiar to users from the technologies they use in their personal lives. But that accessibility and simplicity are deceiving. Take adoption—the number of people signed up on the platform—and engagement—how active they are on the platform. Adoption and engagement are critical measures for consumer social tools because they are vital statistics for advertisers. But they don't measure a tool's utility in an enterprise. There, they show only that "the patient is getting treatment" and is logged on to the system. What they don't convey is the patient's condition or whether the treatment is working—i.e., what, if any, business value the system offers. Just because people are able to use a social application does not necessarily mean it provides value to the organization.

User activity may be high—but who's to know whether users are actually accomplishing anything?

Not Connecting Social to a Business Problem

Unfortunately, many haphazard implementations are causing a backlash against social business. Deloitte explains that senior executives are skeptical of social software, claiming that social evangelists have failed to effectively communicate how social software can drive real operating benefits.[1] Gartner has predicted that through 2015 80 percent of social business efforts will not achieve their intended benefits due to inadequate leadership and overemphasis on technology.[2] Finally, McKinsey found that 65 percent of companies have deployed at least one social software tool[3] but, based on early results, most of these enterprise social deployments will fail to deliver meaningful results.

What these failed projects share is a lack of connection between the technology and the business problem. They covet the value that will be evident when everyone is fully engaged with the platform—the wall-to-wall implementation—but lack a coherent plan for how to get there. "Let's do it!" they say. But first they need to look carefully at their own specific situation. Like the Red Queen, who gives an order without giving a thought to how it is to be accomplished, some firms don't realize that an enterprise-wide solution involves several successful implementations for specific use cases.

Technology alone won't solve a company's problems. If a business is broken, bringing in a social platform won't fix it. If the business's strategy is nonexistent, introducing a social platform will not magically create a strategy. If a company is not clear on what it is trying to accomplish or how it will measure progress, the best social technology in the world cannot ensure success.

Companies must think clearly about intentions and goals. What specific value could be gained by using a social business platform to solve business problems? The technology can do so much more than provide an activity stream where people can post instead of using e-mail. Instead, the activity stream can be used to develop an RFP, close a sale, or pull together a product brochure. That's its selling proposition. When a company takes this approach and emphasizes value over adoption, a company vastly increases its chances for success. But without a clear connection between the social business initiative and a business problem, too many observers will see social technology as just another shiny object.

BEGINNING WITH A PILOT

The words "We're going to do a pilot of a new technology" can seal a project's fate as a failure. Skeptical participants know that a project is a pilot, so they start to bet on its demise. Ignoring the rollout, they keep quiet on the sidelines. And simply by not participating, they actually have a hand in the pilot's failure. Many employees don't intentionally try to kill the pilot; they just don't invest in a project they think is going to fail.

Experiment with a Wave Instead

One way to avoid this dismal situation is to frame an implementation to a functional group or workgroup as the "first priority rollout" or "first wave." (In Chapter 5, we explain how one company used this method.) This signals that the first implementation is the beginning of a longer process, not a test. It also gets potential participants excited about the project. It can even create competition between groups to be part of the initial implementation. The process has the potential to change everything. The first wave must address an existing problem within the business. The participants in the first wave should understand why they were selected, what they will use the platform for, and what process/systems it replaces in their current world.

ALLOWING IT TO RUN ALL
ASPECTS OF A SOCIAL PROJECT

IT departments own most technology purchases, including infrastructure like enterprise data storage and security software, because these solutions solve technology problems. IT departments will also own the social business platform and might manage the rollout. If the project is to succeed, however, the IT department should not determine how and where employees use it or be the group responsible for its success; this is the job of business executives. IT leaders and business executives must partner with each other. Together, they can agree on intent, determine which business challenge the project addresses, and then establish clear targets for success.

FOCUSING ON INTEGRATIONS AT THE EXPENSE OF THE BUSINESS CASE

Steven Kahl, associate professor at the Tuck School of Business at Dartmouth and an expert on technology in the enterprise, explains that integration requirements are one of the differentiators between social software and ERP. Consulting, specifically systems integrations, has traditionally been part of every ERP project. In today's economic environment, firms are "less willing to spend a lot on integration."[4]

Despite these financial constraints, some enterprises begin a social business software project with a long list of proposed integrations. When IT leads an implementation, the team often focuses on interoperability with every other system while deemphasizing the technology's intent. Not only is this unnecessary but it frustrates users who still remember the pain of ERP rollouts. Instead, enterprises should take an incremental approach to integrations. Focus first on the integrations with systems that impact the business case. Take sales enablement, for example: here, priority integrations are sales force automation, e-mail systems, and calendar apps. Other systems, ERP content management and the like, can wait.

USING CONSUMER SOCIAL TOOLS FOR ENTERPRISE COLLABORATION

Consumer Tools Support Business-to-Consumer Communication

Marketers in every industry realize that they must meet customers where they frequently show up: online. Business-to-consumer (B2C) firms focus on Facebook, Twitter, or even Pinterest rather than force customers to an external site. B2C firms use these consumer social networks to connect with existing and potential customers. They run campaigns on the sites and leverage the power of friends/connections to push users to purchase a product or try a service. It's convenient; using Facebook for this project is much simpler and cheaper than setting up a dedicated social network. But while Facebook or Twitter might work to connect a cookie brand to customers, you can't just take a consumer social solution as-is and expect it support either business-to-business (B2B) communication or employee collaboration.

Using a consumer tool for B2B communications can interfere with employees' personal communications. Here's a case in point: Customer service representatives at a financial services firm interact with subscribers on Facebook. In this capacity, these reps represent the company rather than individuals. But what if, as individuals, they want a Facebook account? How do they manage this? What if individuals are fired from the financial services firm? How does the employer disconnect them from Facebook or disassociate them from the company? And, when they communicate, are they communicating as an employee or as an individual? When employees use a consumer social network for personal as well as professional communications, it sets the company up for personnel lawsuits and makes it hard to control corporate data.

B2C Social Platforms Aren't Enterprise Ready

What a B2B firm demands from a social business platform is different from what a B2C company needs. Namely, if a B2B firm is going use it for collaboration, the platform must be enterprise ready. The B2B firm needs control over the social platform. At the same time, the platform needs to integrate with other platforms, support data retention, and uphold security standards. Consumer social tools are great at connecting people but not at enabling them to get work done. After all, they don't provide the integration to the enterprise and uphold the standards that businesses require. Why would they?

Being enterprise ready means supporting functions and roles in an organization, not just individual users. In the consumer world, users act as individuals. On a social business platform, they are representatives of companies. They are filling roles that will exist whether or not the person doing the job continues in the job.

Consider a fictional B2B software company called Valuetech. Valuetech sets up a social business platform for marketing design and execution of its software for financial services firms. Valuetech's goal is to reduce the product's marketing costs and increase revenue. Valuetech customers—financial analysts and their IT teams—and potential customers go to the platform to interact with Valuetech product managers and learn about some of the key features, short-cuts, and valuable add-ons. Valuetech manages the community, interacts directly with customers, and learns which new features to add to the next release.

When a large financial services firm, Market High Research, wants to buy software from Valuetech, Market High's employees go to Valuetech's customer social platform. Market High security analysts can evaluate Valuetech's software based on others' experiences and the discussions on the social business platform. Analysts discuss which features are especially useful as well as best practices for mobile use.

Each Market High employee who engages on the platform develops a relationship with Valuetech and with other community members. Take, Maria, a Market High analyst who participates in Valuetech's customer platform. Valuetech's community manager engages directly with Maria and provides the information Maria needs to run her campaign.

What happens when Maria leaves Market High for Jefferson Funds, and Market High backfills Maria's position with another analyst? This could create a big problem in normal circumstances. But a social business software platform maintains content and context. Even though Maria leaves Market High, her conversations with other users and with Valuetech employees remain on the community platform. Her replacement is quickly productive in the new job because s/he—and anyone else on the platform who has the ability to see this information—can access Maria's conversations and past actions forever. Forever!

This ends the largely prevalent but far less helpful protocol where Maria's e-mails forward to her replacement for a specified period of time. (This is all very well, except that the replacement has no clue which e-mails s/he must read and respond to and which s/he can ignore.) Instead, the new analyst just logs on to the social business platform and sees all of the conversations between Valuetech's team and Maria. An elegant solution!

Similarly, if Valuetech's partner community manager leaves Valuetech, Valuetech doesn't have to piece together conversations that took place between the community manager, employees, and customers. The community manager leaves, but any content s/he created and the conversations s/he had remain. The part of the company's history that s/he represents is not lost. Valuetech doesn't have to worry about users from companies like Market High and Jefferson Funds becoming frustrated because the new Valuetech community manager doesn't understand the history of their accounts. And Valuetech runs a much lower risk of losing sales or angering customers because the social business platform enables Valuetech to provide continuity to customers.

Imagine, instead, if Valuetech used Facebook for B2B interaction. Valuetech would have no means to stop former employees from continuing to communicate with customers. After leaving Valuetech, the former employee would still be able to connect with customers via Facebook or, worse, criticize the former employer directly to customers.

But it's not just about damage control. It's more profound because all of the community manager conversations with customers would leave with him/her. Valuetech would have no control over these conversations because they would take place on Facebook's network, not the social business platform that Valuetech runs, moderates, and maintains. If the community manager was particularly good at solving customers' issues, so much so that his/her coworkers turned to him/her for help when they couldn't find answers, how would Valuetech retain his/her product and service knowledge when s/he left the company? Every interaction on Valuetech's Facebook page would be far inferior until the new community manager got up to speed. But beyond not offering the same level of service, Valuetech would be unable to fulfill compliance and legal obligations. If the conversations took place on a platform where Valuetech didn't own the data, it would be unable to reproduce these conversations as needed.

USING A FREE PRODUCT AS A DE FACTO SOLUTION

Enterprise workers struggled for years to get the tools they wanted. With the advent of cloud, individuals gain direct access to software without involving IT. Users can pick and choose applications without IT's approval.

Freemium software (where a basic/lite version is free but the premium version requires payment) is a common type of software accessible through the cloud. At one organization, employees might use various cloud storage solutions—Google Drive, Dropbox, Windows SkyDrive, etc.—to store files. Users might find it annoying to have to access several different services to retrieve a file, but ultimately, they find the file they need.

While freemium software can be great for document management and storage needs, freemium collaboration software isn't optimal for enterprise use. Freemium works well when the user/buyer is the same person and can determine the value and the features s/he needs. The problem in a collaborative scenario is that a single user cannot determine comprehensive user requirements for the enterprise. The purchaser and the many, many individuals who will use the platform are different and have many different needs. Further, though users can share documents from several different cloud-based file storage systems, a collaboration platform only works if everyone is on the same platform. If individual users are downloading different types of freemium collaboration software, who makes the decision about which tool they will use going forward? Everyone in the enterprise must agree on which collaboration platform to use and, when enough people in the organization adopt it, IT must monitor usage, security, and compliance. It's another layer of complexity.

Free Products Make Companies Nervous

IT departments are often skeptical of free software; they think it's free for a shady reason, i.e., it is missing functionality or has some other flaw. As Greg D'Alesandre, former senior product marketing manager for Google Wave, explains, "When a company pays for a product, they have confidence that the company isn't going to just yank it away."[5] Similarly, Ian MacLeod, an industry veteran and technology banker, cautions:

> Though freemium businesses are expanding rapidly, in the enterprise, people are used to paying for value. In fact, they feel better if they pay for it. It means the vendor has an obligation to the enterprise buyer. Without paying, there is no obligation.

In the enterprise, it is all about service. With service level agreements (SLAs), you know what you are paying for and what you get for that fee. Consumers don't care about these agreements—they don't need an SLA around Twitter. If something is mission critical, however, enterprises are willing to pay for it. For businesses, the ability to communicate and collaborate is mission critical.[6]

TRYING TO MAKE THE OLD NEW AGAIN

Many application vendors add social functionality to an existing product and often enterprises try to make do with these enhanced products. But bolting on social to an application designed for a different task—say, document management—isn't easy. D'Alesandre believes that companies that take an existing social technology, put an enterprise brand on it, and sell it as enterprise software follow a strategy that cannot provide long-term value to enterprises.[7] These solutions lack connections to intranets, integration to enterprise search applications, and links to content management and document management systems.

"Social" is not a goal in and of itself. It is a new way of doing traditional business activities more effectively. Organizations that say, "Now we're social" leave themselves no way to assess the value of social technology. Just because they use a product with an activity stream doesn't mean they are social. An activity stream can be a feature of a social business platform, but alone, it's just a list of events.

Using SharePoint as a Social Tool

SharePoint has historically been a process management, document storage, and small team collaboration tool. At these tasks, public opinion says SharePoint works. In fact, companies often use SharePoint as the path of least resistance for collaboration.

When users in business functions, many of whom had had access to SharePoint, heard the story of stand-alone social business platforms, they were intrigued. They went to IT and asked for the software only to hear, "Another new platform? We don't know if we are going to look into a new platform. It would need to be integrated into our current systems. We have Microsoft SharePoint, and they are, supposedly, rolling out something just like what you want."

For companies that have already invested heavily in a product, it's hard to ignore sunk costs. Many companies continue to use SharePoint, even when better solutions exist because they already have product experts on staff. But when you architect a people-centric social collaboration platform on top of an application that was intended for another purpose, the result can be less than stellar. Microsoft built SharePoint for content and document management. To make SharePoint a social platform would require major upgrades of the entire system—a complete overhaul. Instead of just accepting social features on top of SharePoint, companies that want value from a social business platform should opt for a tool that was built for collaboration from the get-go.

The social solutions that have real staying power are built with an understanding of the enterprise. They bake social tech into what the enterprise actually needs. They don't add social features to an existing product, they merge enterprise and social technologies. D'Alesandre explains the difference between these approaches:

> It's similar to transplanting part of a living plant to another plant versus crossbreeding two plants. In many cases, the transplanted plant will die on the vine. The crossbreeding experiment will take longer and be harder to accomplish but, ultimately, have longevity.[8]

The Stack Solution Versus Best-of-Breed Software

Everyone involved in enterprise software is analyzing the market and trying to figure out what the enterprise software stack will look like in 2020. The major players in enterprise software—Oracle, SAP, Microsoft, etc.—position themselves as having all of the functionality that users will want in an integrated suite.

When an enterprise opts for a single vendor stack, it often gets many applications, features, and add-ons that it doesn't want. Think of it like buying a package honeymoon vacation that the travel agent positions as the "best value trip." You get a hotel room, meals, and a walking tour of the town thrown in. If you put together such a vacation on your own, you would have to spend more on food and lodging and ignore the activities that didn't interest you. You probably wouldn't have chosen each element of the trip you're getting—but when it's free, you opt in.

Similarly, it's tempting to go for it when a vendor comes in, offers a discount, and throws in social features for free. The problem is, you get what you pay for. You don't know what to do with the free social features; you never evaluated them and didn't have a plan for how you'd use them. If you try to use them, they might simply turn out to be a waste of your time.

While it might still be time-consuming to plan your holiday piece-by-piece, it's becoming a lot easier to build and manage a best-of-breed stack with vendors like Jive, Okta, Workday, and Box. Simple application programming interfaces make combining point solutions easy; it's no longer an IT headache. Users often get a better product that is focused around a specific value proposition. Small companies are agile, fast, and often more responsive to customer needs. And, because these best-of-breed providers have to be 10 times better than next best product, they are causing massive disruption.

Content Accessibility Does Not Equal Content Availability

Enterprises have overinvested in content management. They have massive file sharing systems that are very expensive to implement and maintain. Scott Johnston, director of product management for Google Drive, explains that content management systems' requirements are laborious and time-consuming for the user, too. A person has to fill in 27 fields to upload a document.[9] They may be able to store large amounts of data, but working with them is complicated. Firms need other solutions, specifically simple cloud-based applications.

Cloud solutions, while seemingly offering enterprises less control, embody content availability. Though skeptics hear the words "file sharing" and "sync" and assume that security/data exposure will be worse than what they have with their existing solution, e-mailing and downloading files between users is just as insecure. With cloud storage products like Google Drive or Box, data sharing is secure and controlled. Cloud storage makes it possible for users to have five-9s availability (the system is available 99.999 percent of the time), work locally, and sync data in the cloud.[10]

ASSUMING SOCIAL BUSINESS SOFTWARE IS ONLY FOR THE MARKETING DEPARTMENT

Andy Sernovitz, author of *Word of Mouth Marketing: How Smart Companies Get People Talking*, says one mistake companies make is they put social business software in the marketing bucket and then measure the impact on sales. He cautions that "Social is not a direct marketing channel." Nevertheless, many companies see social as a conversation channel and jam it with advertising.[11] Social is no longer just a tactic to master for marketing; it is a change driver for every department.

Social business is clearly in the early stages of its maturity. But it is already finding its way to the mainstream buyer. Executives and IT buyers must cut through all of the vendors and find those companies that are both strong today and promise to last into the future. According to a recent report by McKinsey Global Institute, companies that wait to implement social technologies put themselves at a disadvantage:

> The benefits of social technologies will likely outweigh the
> risks for most companies. Organizations that fail to invest in
> understanding social technologies will be at greater risk of
> having their business models disrupted by social technologies.[12]

That's a paradox worth contemplating.

CHAPTER 7

THE UNRESOLVED ISSUES

THE STUMBLING BLOCKS BEFORE THE CLOUD

When software-as-a-service began, companies feared they'd expose themselves to risks if they adopted SaaS solutions. Choosing SaaS over on-premise software meant relinquishing customization. Worse, it meant relinquishing control.

But with experience, the outlook has changed. Once companies experience how easy and fast it is to get software delivered from the cloud, including dynamic upgrades, they become believers. In the face of SaaS simplicity, they realize that customization was never as simple as they had hoped. In light of that fact, they conclude they'd prefer to swap some customization for simplicity and flexibility.

Of course there are companies that still hesitate moving to the cloud to access applications, computing resources, and platforms. For those firms, seamless delivery of innovation will be a forcing mechanism. A firm that has to manage its own upgrades and installations won't be able to keep pace with enterprises that get all their technology as a service. On-premise will lose traction when vendors stop supporting noncloud products.

The replacement cycle will affect even the largest and most expensive technology deployments; IT will start replacing traditional on-premise enterprise apps from vendors like Oracle and SAP with cloud-based versions. Eventually, every division and every company will receive version updates simultaneously—even without being aware of it.

Today, most enterprises take a silo approach to social business platforms and limit collaboration to internal users. But this doesn't offer the biggest benefits. When an enterprise accesses most of its data and applications from the cloud, it gains the ability to combine its networks in secure ways.

THE NEED FOR SOCIAL STANDARDS

While the move to the cloud is almost inevitable, what isn't clear is who will manage connections between different cloud systems. Uncontrolled virality between social business systems is a real risk unless a body steps forward to manage roles, authentication, and permissions. Like every other communication network from telephone to e-mail, until social standards exist, a common communication network won't arise.

As social business platforms become more valuable and mature, the lack of social business software standards will emerge as an issue. The industry will need to agree on how enterprise applications connect to social applications and enterprise social platforms connect to each other.

A History of Communications Standards

By the early 1900s, AT&T had become a major player in telecommunications. AT&T had bought several Bell-associated companies, independents, and also control of Western Union. AT&T refused to connect its long-distance network with local independent carriers, hurting both the small carriers and consumers. In 1907, AT&T claimed that the telephone, by its nature, would operate most efficiently as a monopoly providing universal service. The U.S.

government accepted this principle and granted this monopoly in a 1913 agreement known as the Kingsbury Commitment.

Under the Kingsbury Commitment, AT&T could connect independent telephone companies to the AT&T network. This gave AT&T an advantage over smaller firms and potential new entrants, but helped push the concept of universal telephone service. The percentage of American households with telephone service reached 90 percent by 1969.[1]

When e-mail became widespread in the early 1990s, messages only traveled in closed systems. People e-mailed internal colleagues, but many e-mail systems didn't accept messages from people outside the company. Once the standard SMTP (simple mail transfer protocol) was introduced, e-mail could flow between organizations. SMTP also gave rise to an industry around e-mail by spurring e-mail providers, e-mail clients, and e-mail services firms.

Preliminary Social Standards

OpenSocial, a standard for web-based social applications launched in 2007, is guiding the development of social applications. The standard began in the consumer social space, but until recently, it hasn't had significant traction in enterprise social applications. What's unique about OpenSocial is that, unlike other open standards like RSS, OpenSocial supports two-way data exchange.

Companies that developed transactional systems are now trying to map their software into social business software systems. They realize that despite all the investment they've made to ERP and the like, these systems only capture 10 to 20 percent of what's happening in a business. OpenSocial increases the power of social business software by enabling social platforms to bring data from transactional systems—CRM, Salesforce, or ERP—into social systems. In doing so, OpenSocial helps fulfill the ultimate promise of social business software as a platform for the enterprise.

The lack of specific standards for today's social business software systems limits these systems' utility. For instance, if a person is working at Toyota and wants to work with an engineer at Delphi, a leading automotive parts manufacturer, he can invite the engineer to the Toyota partner social business platform. But if Delphi already has its own social business platform, it would be easier for the two platforms to work together directly rather than making the Delphi engineer join yet another network. Open standards could make this collaboration simpler.

As social business software moves from early adoption to mainstream, open standards will gain importance. Further, when buyers know that a social platform implements open standards, they have more confidence in the platform. Critical mass drives interoperability; these standards will take off when social business vendors and users widely support them.

Data Communication and Ownership Misalignment

In the cloud, information owners and service providers can conflict. Users store documents on everything from Google Drive to Microsoft SkyDrive to Dropbox to Box, yet they can't share files between these cloud services. Information owners, the users, want that information to be free to travel between different systems. In contrast, storage providers eschew this idea. They want control over when and how data can travel. If vendors can't keep these services closed, how do they show their unique values and distinguish themselves?

As Matt Tucker, founder of Jive Software, explains:

> Fighting open standards is a way to protect an ecosystem.
> Monolithic enterprise providers don't like open standards
> because they make it hard to achieve vendor lock-in. But it's a
> world where a single vendor can't cut it anymore; a world where
> new disruptive technologies appear all the time. The notion of
> single stack is antiquated.[2]

Companies that provide cloud-based solutions have an inherent conflict of interest. We need a compromise in the middle that can both protect the vendors and provide value and simplification to users.

Network Consolidation and Overlap

Sometimes it feels as though a new social network appears daily. While new social networks have the potential to be even more valuable than those that came before, individuals will eventually concede that being on many social networks is more of a burden than an advantage. The value of a network is a power function that increases with each connected node. If networks consolidate, users will be able to centrally manage what shows up in all of these networks.

In the consumer world, we are already seeing consolidation—Facebook buying Instagram is just one such example. In the enterprise, separate social networks (Yammer, Google+, LinkedIn) should be able to intersect with social workspaces like Huddle, Jive, and SharePoint. Until they do, however, users who are active on social business platforms have to manage with five different profiles and inboxes. Most likely, social networks and social workplaces will eventually stitch together seamlessly across the firewall and across value chains. This will make both types of applications more powerful, easier to use, and more valuable for individuals and the organizations where they work.

WORKERS' COUNCILS AND UNIONS AND THE BOUNDARIES OF WORK

Self-organizing workers' groups have been granted many protections by law. To date, these protections have applied to all aspects of workers' activities. Social platforms, however, are a new domain that the previous rules don't cover. They represent a gray area that has yet to be resolved.

Uncertainty around what kinds of work unionized employees do on the platform causes sensitivity when companies are deploying a social business platform.

Some companies are concerned that managers might judge employees based on points they earn on a social platform, rather than on their performance. Second, most unions lack policies as to when and where employees can participate on a social business platform. For instance, can employees log in from home? During this time, they aren't technically on the clock. Does the company have to compensate them for the time they spend on the network outside of work hours? Are employees' actions protected by union rules? What if they connect with peers on the platform? If they engage on the platform by choice, does that not count as work?

We can't answer all of these questions today. Rather, we will need to collectively figure out how to uphold workers' rights without limiting their desire to engage on a social platform and get work done on the platform.

MAINTAINING COMPLIANCE

Social business software is a new area for most companies, and compliance requirements are blurry. In the face of evolving rules, companies and individuals tend to gravitate toward a conservative approach. In some cases, companies choose to shut down social business software rather than risk unknowingly or unlawfully sharing sensitive information.

Issues Around Data Retention

Enterprises want to be able to access their data quickly and easily. When a company hosts its own software and has all data on site, finding information isn't too difficult. For instance, when a company does e-discovery, the process of uncovering electronic information for civil litigation, finding e-mails is straightforward. Security specialists are starting to use similar data vaults for social content and plan to keep it accessible for e-discovery.

Passive Participation

What complicates data retention and e-discovery is that some participation on a social business platform is passive. The application can track who contributed to a forum or "liked" a video, but it can't show if someone just viewed a piece of content. Some issues around data retention are uncertain and lack rules.

Data Destruction

Many federal agencies and contractors won't buy software unless they can physically destroy data. They even go so far as to use a sledgehammer or shredder to smash a disk drive. But cloud-based vendors don't offer physical drive destruction as a service. Moreover, with modern data replication across clouds, this kind of data destruction has become a quaint concept.

Some SaaS vendors do have a policy of retaining data for 90 days post–user deletion. After 90 days, they remove all local and all backup copies of deleted data. While it isn't physical destruction of a disk drive, this process is sufficient for a majority of customers, including financial firms. Many social business software vendors also back up data on encrypted hardware filers managed by a third party.

Data Privacy and Compliance in Regulated Industries

Despite these obvious concerns, some of the most successful implementations of social business software have been in the financial services industry. These companies have straddled two worlds—they want to keep things locked down for security but also favor open communication to engage employees and increase efficiency. Transparency is overtaking security concerns. Increasingly, financial institutions are realizing that everything from cost cutting to innovation to getting work done happens more easily if they can get employees working together.

FINRA and Compliance Overview

In 2009, the Financial Industry Regulatory Authority released Regulatory Notice 10–06[3] detailing guidelines on communications for blogs and social networking websites. These regulations include:

Archive

All communications via social networks must be retained.

Supervise

Employees must receive training on the firm's written policies and procedures before engaging in social media. Static content must be pre-approved by the firm, while real-time interactive communications need to be "supervised."

Include Disclaimers

Although not required, it is recommended to add a disclaimer to remove any doubt about the organization's affiliation with third-party opinions expressed within the social media platform.

Avoid Recommendations

Company representatives should not advise or endorse financial investments via social media. Warning: This *does* apply to the "Like" feature on Facebook, and retweeting on Twitter, both of which could be considered entanglement.[4]

In financial services, mergers and acquisitions specifically, companies maintain a separation between investment research and banking, by law. It follows that prospective social technology users in financial services worry about housing both of these departments in the same community. These fears are legitimate but easy to address. First, they ignore the fact that these groups are already communicating both formally and informally. Secondly, a robust social business system can include both public and secret areas, integrate existing systems (CRM, ERP, etc.), and unite them with strong security features that other systems lack. These features enable banking and research teams to work together on one social business system and keep certain topics private, while keeping public topics—a new human resources policy, thoughts on the market, and compensation—public.

Case Study: Global Bank

One global bank that implemented a social business platform was concerned about how it would separate research analysts and investment bankers. As a percent of the bank's total workforce, these groups comprised very few people and were among the least likely individuals to use the software.

The bank simplified the implementation to account for compliance concerns. When the bank implemented the social business platform in the United States, it opened up the platform to everyone except investment bankers and research analysts. During the first six months of the implementation, the rest of the bank could learn how the software worked and how it applied to their work. People working in support functions, such as IT, operations, and human resources, became heavy users. Though employees were worried about others talking about clients, posting inappropriately, or sharing private information, none of these things happened.

As John Stepper, a managing director focused on collaboration and social media tools at the bank, recalls, "We solved the 90 percent problem first." They took what Stepper calls, "a big enough step without touching their biggest concerns." Only at the end of 2012 did the firm include bankers and research as read-only users.[5] The bank found a way to make employees more comfortable by taking the most awful fears about data security and privacy they could imagine, and putting them on the table.

The implementation team explained that all the information on the system is retained, not in the cloud but on the bank's servers. If people see content that they think is inappropriate, they just click a button to send it to the moderator. In the meantime, the community manager removes the content. As more employees experiment with the tool, the company gains evidence of the tool's security.

Case Study: UBS

UBS found a way to implement social business software in a highly regulated environment. First, they modified the tool's retention module to meet most of the U.S. government security requirements as well as the requirements of other governments across the globe. They also limited the type of data that users could put on the system—for example, they don't allow confidential or client information of any kind. UBS opted for a 100 percent on-premise solution in order to meet its security standards and connect with legacy archiving systems.

As Scott Ross, executive director of IT research and development, explains, even with these limitations, the system is still useful:

The organization that can collaborate most efficiently and effectively across geographies, products and organizational teams, both internally and externally, will deliver superior solutions to their clients and shareholders. Our business vision is to put the client at the center of everything we do. Social is a key enabler for us achieving this vision both inside and outside our franchise.[6]

Case Study: Mutual Fund Company

When a large mutual fund company introduced a social business platform to its employees, the company, understandably, had concerns about security controls and access to customer data. To start, the financial services firm's own security procedures were more stringent than those of many firms; it didn't allow employees' machines to enable USB ports and limited employees' Internet access. Even so, the company chose a hosted, off-premise social business software solution.

Securing a cloud-based social business platform to the company's standards seemed like an impossible requirement. Rather than focusing heavily on matching the company's on-premise security specifications (especially since many could be circumvented with cloud applications and scripts), the vendor focused on understanding the customer's real concern: pro-tecting data and controlling who touches the data. The vendor introduced a new monitoring system that took log feeds from several sources and correlated them to the system. Anytime someone touched data for specific types of activity, the system

> notified the company. In addition to its standard security pro-
> cedure, the vendor gave the company a SOC level 2 report,
> which documented how it monitored access to the environment
> and data and allowed the mutual fund firm to audit the cloud
> environment.

Similarly, organizations like healthcare agencies and credit card issuers that must adhere to state and Payment Card Industry (PCI) privacy laws almost always fear users sharing personal information like credit card numbers and social security numbers on the system. Their concern about PCI on a social business platform, however, is no different from previous concerns about putting this information in e-mails. In the case of a social business platform, though, the SaaS vendor can write scripts to block certain data. Ultimately, security comes down to the enterprises instituting good security practices internally. It is the job of community managers to monitor usage and data and set up user agreements.

Data Security on Hosted Applications

One security issue that is still unresolved is the technology vendor's access to customer data. The vendor that hosts an application can gain access to the client data on the system; the vendor can't adequately support customers without access to their data. Even if the vendor were to monitor who touches the data, it could still find a way to cover up any unlawful use of customer data. Today, vendors offer many procedures and legal agreements that protect this type of arrangement. In the future, we will need to make new agreements to govern data access in these situations.

Intermingling Customer Data

Mixing different customers' data is another security issue that social technology buyers fear. To circumvent this issue, some large firms build their own cloud. Banks have their own clouds because they need to be able to find the source of a problem if their network goes down. When a company does choose a public cloud, the cloud provider can mitigate security concerns about data separation with identification controls, authentication, etc. While it is ostensibly riskier than putting all data on proprietary systems, today's new technology and security processes are progressively minimizing risk. To control access to data, the system gives tenet IDs to all users. Even if a cloud intermingles data from different sources, at API/software level, users can't access any data without the tenet ID.

Though independent security auditors are becoming more common, securing data is moving from a general trust issue to a more routine and sophisticated process. The expectation is that as the platform matures, it will build in more control for flow of information. While social business platforms introduce new vulnerabilities, as they mature they will uphold security standards that exceed those of e-mail or private corporate networks.

CUSTOMIZATION

Multitenancy—hosting several customers in one cloud—has cost and performance advantages, but also drawbacks. Think about Google's commuter bus that takes 50 employees from San Francisco to Mountain View. It's far cheaper for passengers and better for the environment. You can even work on the bus!

But passengers do make some sacrifices. They all have to ride in the same environment: the same heating and air conditioning, the same driver, and a strict pickup and drop-off schedule. Still, most feel that the sacrifices are worth the benefits.

Similarly, a cloud-based application provider runs one version of the software and has one data store. The vendor can roll out new features to all users at any time, which means users always access the latest version of an application. Enterprises don't have to provide as much on-site support to users, pay for maintenance, allocate resources for data storage, or manage security. But efficiency comes with a price. To avoid slowing down the system with testing and independent upgrades, the provider must limit some customization.

MANAGING AND LEADING IN
A TRANSPARENT WORLD

An important but more amorphous unresolved issue relates to cultural norms and leadership. Social business platforms and social intranets, in particular, open a window—or rather, a door—to discussions that once took place only between specific groups. In many cases, these discussions weren't private because they contained sensitive information, but because participants either assumed that the larger company wouldn't be interested in the discussion, or firms lacked a way to efficiently include outsiders without overloading e-mail boxes, or they didn't know who to include in the discussion.

Even CEOs, who naturally manage high levels of transparency with investors and the press, are not always good at communicating with employees. They may lack the time or an appropriate forum. But when a CEO contributes on a social business platform, s/he can connect with employees and customers on a more personal level. Executives get credit for those instances when they make mistakes. When these leaders show they're human, their employees are more likely to forgive them.

Social technologies are not about giving the illusion that we listen and are engaged. Companies are learning that they need to engage with their customers more proactively. Businesses are seeing they need to authentically engage with their employees. Social provides the means to make this possible and scalable.

Depending on an employee's age, her/his view on using a social business platform will vary. Millennials grew up in an age of transparency. They are accustomed to sharing everything about their lives, but they haven't yet seen many of the train wrecks that result when private information is made public. On the flip side, those who grew up in a more private world are more wary; they have habits that are hard to break and reputations to lose if something goes wrong.

Enterprises balk at making all company information public; transparency changes the internal power structure in organizations. In many firms, executives own a disproportionate share of the information. They know when the company will expand, what new product it will offer, or which divisions will be cut. Further down, middle managers translate information between the people who are on the front lines of the business and the top layer of management. This is an ideal arrangement for managers who don't believe all employees should be privy to all conversations in a company, whether for a "need to know" or because of a "lack of context" mentality.

Power shifts when everyone has access to more information and a means to share that information. Well-informed employees start questioning the status quo. They ask, "I heard the CEO say x," or "Why aren't we doing this?"

Jesper Sørensen, professor of organizational behavior at Stanford Graduate School of Business, describes how transparency changes power dynamics:

> Social software makes transparent an enterprise's informal structure and, in the process, can weaken the ability of certain individuals to be roadblocks. These "network entrepreneurs" had ensured that the important information flowed through them. Social business software democratizes information flow and makes firms less dependent on these specific individuals.[7]

The benefit of more democratic information flow is that an organization's mission comes closer to those people responsible for execution. A new corporate strategy becomes possible, allowing the firm to get critical information to everyone in the organization, not just executives or network entrepreneurs.

Instituting Communication Rules

Organizations that worry that employees will access inappropriate information on the social platform can manage behavior by making the standards for participation clear. A social business system can be configured to remind users, upon login, that it is a business system.

It's harder to be anonymous on a social business platform than on a consumer social network. Unlike a consumer social network like Twitter, usernames can't be disguised. Employees are less likely to flame other users or say something uncouth if their coworkers can easily identify them as the content creator.

Social business platforms can also build in controls that allow anyone in the organization to click and flag content for moderation and removal, if necessary. This makes damage control much more immediate and effective. On e-mail, users have no way of recalling content—it's impossible to retrieve an e-mail from thousands of distributed e-mail boxes.

CONTROLLING USAGE

After witnessing how engrossing Facebook and other consumer social networks can be, some companies fear that giving employees access to an enterprise social platform is a mistake. They worry that workers will spend all day reading or commenting on the platform and not get any work done. But based on what we've seen in several industries, concern about people whiling away the day is unfounded. You might have an initial burst of engagement, but people get back to their jobs. They learn to use the platform to do their work more effectively.

DETERMINING OPTIMAL ADOPTION TIME

The Early Adopters

Some firms choose to be early adopters of new technologies. They want to be on the cutting edge of change and innovation. Even if the technology isn't perfect, they'll tailor it to their needs, as Scott Johnston, director of product management for Google Drive, explains:

> Early adopters differentiate themselves with flexible and agile IT departments. These IT groups see themselves as providing solutions to people to get things done, not gatekeepers who stop employees from adopting new technologies. They don't have a lockdown mentality; they want to look at all the technology options available.[8]

The Pitfalls of Early Adoption: Google Wave

The risk of early adoption is you may bet on a failure.

One of the earliest social business applications, Google Wave, may have faltered because Google was early to an undeveloped market. Google launched Wave, a real-time messaging and collaboration platform, in September 2009. The product was "part e-mail, part Twitter and part instant messaging."[9] It combined e-mail, instant messaging, wikis, web chat, social networking, and project management in an elegant, in-browser communication client. It enabled both discussions and online file sharing for consumer and business users. Speculators even imagined that Wave could redefine web communications.

The product showed promise, but the company struggled to explain Wave to the public. Gmail was web e-mail; GoogleDocs was an online tool for creating and sharing documents. Wave had no clear metaphor. Google took a long time to launch Wave, thus frustrating users and hurting momentum. Finally, critics claimed Wave's final product simply wasn't very good.[10]

Google killed the product but only after some users had already adopted it. Novell wanted to be an early Wave adopter and built Pulse, an enterprise-focused collaboration tool, using the Google Wave Federation Protocol. Unfortunately, Novell made these investments in vain. Novell and other early adopters jumped in too soon.

Lack of Sector Leadership

Firms might delay implementing a social business platform because they're waiting for an industry shakeout. The landscape is scattered with companies whose products fall under a larger definition of social software but offer very different solutions. Mergers and acquisitions are happening, and this makes buyers wary. Analysts have been tracking the social business software space for approximately six years, yet no one technology solution merges all of the great features of each offering and gains widespread adoption.

Enterprises don't want to make a commitment to a product only to find that the software maker goes out of business or gets acquired or absorbed into a larger product. In fact, some companies will only buy from a public company in order to avoid obsolescence. Socialcast and CubeTree both had promise, but then VMware and SuccessFactors, respectively, acquired them. Blogtronix (renamed Sharetronix in May 2012) was an early social appliance. The company had some success with a few media companies but ultimately disappeared from the landscape. In 2012, Microsoft purchased Yammer for the hefty sum of $1.2 billion, even though Yammer had an immature business. It had reached only $20 to $25 million in revenue in 2011.[11]

The market has as many possible futures as it does contenders.

Companies that wait until a technology becomes commoditized before adopting it might miss out on some of the pain. At the front end of the ERP rollouts, companies destroyed billions of dollars of business value by botching implementations.

Managing the moment when you enter on the risk scale is a personal exercise, but waiting too long is an exercise in suicide. While social business platforms are still evolving, the alignment between technology and need has reached a point where companies cannot ignore the opportunity to use a social business platform to drive business value.

THE IT DEPARTMENT IS A ROADBLOCK TO CHANGE, NOT A PARTNER

In some cases, an organization may be ready for a social business platform but IT is a bottleneck. Corporate IT departments are managing multiple projects. They have no time to evaluate new technologies. When an employee asks about a social business platform, IT replies that it will take six months before IT will be able to do an evaluation. Meanwhile, the pace of change continues to accelerate. The business side of the enterprise cannot wait for IT to catch up. A user goes to the software maker's site, gives her credit card, and starts using the application she needs.

How did IT become a roadblock to change? When the office of the CIO (chief information officer) came to power in the 1990s, technology was a strategic enabler. Enterprises started collecting many kinds of systems and applications, some extremely useful and some not. To rationalize all of these investments and secure their own positions, CIOs started to work on administrative tasks like compliance and cost control. Before long, CIOs were reporting to the CFO and were as focused on controlling costs as they were on strategic enablement.

The bring-your-own-device movement challenged IT help desks. Support technicians were nervous about providing answers to a variety of questions. They couldn't be sure that everyone on their team would be able to debug a wide range of applications or troubleshoot multiple devices. Personal computers and mobile devices, IT explained, would compromise security and spread viruses. PCs had security protection including software to manage the machine and patch security holes and encryption to make the data inaccessible if the machine was lost. But security management for new mobile devices was in its infancy. If a person lost the device, all of the content would be exposed.

IT had no way to prevent data from workers' mobile devices from coming into the enterprise, nor any means to wipe them if users put corporate data on them and then later misplaced them. IT groups couldn't control what employees were doing on their devices, yet they were still responsible for compliance and security. Corporate IT departments warned that the company could be fined by the SEC if private customer information got in the hands of someone outside the company.

This wasn't a new problem. The difference was that with mobile devices, old tactics were no longer effective. Enterprises had fewer control points; ad hoc and blunt security solutions no longer worked. Consider the story a longtime computer security expert told about a government contractor's frustration when employees brought their own devices to work. This firm issued each person on the IT staff a glue gun and sent them around the world to various offices, as the enterprise security expert recounted:

> The members of the IT staff were instructed to use hot glue to cover every PC's open ports. They blocked access to USB ports, fat wire ports, etc. and made it impossible for a worker to attach

any media device to their machine. This was the company's strategy to halt progress and stop employees from using devices. You could feel the pressure. The extremes that companies would reach to manage and protect company technology were amazing.[12]

It was, the security expert recalls, a perfect storm:

If you were a security IT person, you had major vectors—an increase in malicious software ("malware"), the consumerization of IT, and greater numbers of employees wanting to bring their own devices (BYOD) to connect to cloud-based software applications, increasing access to all types of social media and social applications.

Today, companies need strategic-minded CIOs who understand that the "bring your own device" trend is not going away yet can still figure out a way to maintain data security. CIOs must fully comprehend the new landscape and capabilities rather than just paint by numbers.

Security in the cloud feels like a trade-off—control for collaboration. Enterprises are trying to find a middle ground. They are reevaluating their security requirements and delineating between information that truly needs to be secure vs. situations where gains in efficiency override security concerns. For instance, companies ask themselves, "How much am I losing if my knowledge workers cannot access this information when they are commuting to work on the train?"

The Way Forward for CIOs

CIOs play a specific role in social business success. Bud Methaisel of PwC suggests that rather than upholding policy and enforcing security rules, evolutionary CIOs must see themselves, again, as strategic enablers. They need to embrace experimentation and find a balance between the extremes of closing the doors to any social technology and flinging the doors too wide open, without any purpose, hoping that the enterprise will achieve something of value.[13]

NEW ISSUES

Social software removes inefficiencies but, in the process, can create new problems. When we talk offline, we can have closed conversations. On a social platform, however, people—if they choose—can make everything they say visible to the entire company. Here, everyone can hear what we say. In fact, a conversation can go on forever, and anyone who wants can chime in to the discussion. Before long, countless debates can't be resolved for the throngs of people involved and, when new people join a platform, they comment on a discussion even when everyone else has moved on.

Fortunately, this problem is solvable by using the features in the software to signal resolution. By taking these threads to termination points and marking outcomes, social software can help companies get work done, make decisions, and drive productivity within the enterprise. It's a subtle shift, but it provides tremendous business value.

RESOLUTION WILL COME

Vendors and governing bodies know of companies' concerns about social business platforms and are addressing these concerns. As these platforms mature and companies transition from on-premise computing to the cloud, we expect new laws to appear that govern usage and put in place new requirements for vendors.

Social business platforms are still in the transitional phase. The concerns and unresolved issues that currently hold enterprises back will sort themselves out. Even in these early days of social business, the best approach is not to wait for these open issues to resolve. Instead, now is the time to start looking seriously at a social business platform.

CHAPTER 8

TIME TO GET STARTED

— BUSINESS ISN'T SLOWING DOWN —

Social business is still at a nascent stage. Firms have so many apparent reasons to resist implementing a social business platform. The reasons sound plausible enough: there's no compelling event to push you into taking this step; you want to wait until the technology matures; the time and expense costs are too high.

While these rationales may seem sensible, here is the case for why you should push beyond them: business is not slowing down, so nor can your company. The first chapter of this book showed how the pace of change is accelerating. It's clear that those companies that wait to implement a social business platform will continue to fall further behind those that started first, even if both groups accelerate at the same speed following an implementation. As the Red Queen would have commented, the slow-off-the-mark company will have to run at least twice as fast to keep up thereafter.

Now is the time to jump on to that chessboard and get started. Several significant milestones have been met that make joining the game a much less risky proposition than ever before.

Technology Maturation

The technology platforms that support social business applications have matured:

- ▶ Many of social business platforms in the space are in their fifth or sixth year of development.
- ▶ Application—programming interfaces (APIs) have been flushed out, integrations are in place, and analytics are now widespread, helping to measure the activity on the system that enterprises care about and bring meaningful insights.
- ▶ Most significantly, social business platforms no longer require extensive customization.

The foundation has been laid; the risk of future costly upgrades due to a substantial re-architecture has passed.

Business Value Is Clear

Social business platforms now have clear value propositions. It's possible to build a business case for implementation and then measure the value that results when people go to the platform to get work done. And, thanks to the proliferation of social technologies in the consumer space, your employees already understand enterprise social technologies—these tools require less explanation than ever before.

The Early Adopters Paved the Way

As we've detailed in this book, enterprises—including Fortune 500 firms and small teams—have gained significant experience in achieving success. They've learned the best practices around defining where in the organization to start, managing the process, and, ultimately, expanding beyond the initial implementation to achieve a wall-to-wall, fully social organization.

A Supportive Ecosystem

Implementation partners have formed a supportive ecosystem around social business application. They have expertise not only in the technologies themselves but also the change management required to adopt these technologies and get clear business value from them.

The risks for investing in social business now are lower than ever before. But start now because it will, ultimately, be a journey. Thousands of micro-transformations will fuel the larger enterprise transformation that is required, though this will take years. The market and vendors will continue to address the challenges identified in the previous chapter including compliance, verticalization, and localization. With the removal of each point of friction, the transformation of all industry will continue to accelerate. Ultimately, all companies will move forward, but some will be ahead and some far behind in the race. Why not be in the vanguard?

STEPS FOR GETTING STARTED

Recalling some critical points from the previous chapters, take note of these steps for heading in a winning direction from the start:

Pick a use case where successful early adopters have consistently proven their ability to clearly create and then measure business value. If IT leads the implementation, make sure they partner with the business owner.

Pick a platform that best enables and supports the use case you have selected. Be mindful of the key criteria for choosing the platform:

- ▶ Purpose–built for your use case
- ▶ Ease of integration into your systems
- ▶ Simple usability by your workers
- ▶ Analytics that show real value
- ▶ Enterprise readiness (scale, security, compliance, localization)
- ▶ Industry proven leadership
- ▶ References from customers you've heard of
- ▶ A true product road map (visionary rather than a backlog of future features)

Build a business case. This is a set of strategic assumptions that help you quantify the value that you hope to achieve. Like a sales plan, the business case is not a guarantee of an outcome. Instead, it's what you believe is an achievable model that guides all subsequent decision making.

Clearly lay out the From>To. Don't just identify your current pain points. You need to also identify the systems that you will limit or remove (e.g., a legacy portal) and then train everyone that will touch the new system how to get work done on the new platform.

Measure, measure, measure and, importantly, share the results.

The Value of the Network Grows with More Nodes

Why is this approach—starting small and adding use cases one-by-one—the best, if what you ultimately want to achieve is the grand vision of the connected company? The grand vision is driven by the power of a social network. As is the case in many networks, Metcalfe's law explains that the value on a social business platform increases as it adds nodes, or users. As the network grows, its power grows proportionally.

This means the riskiest part of the entire journey consists of the first steps.

During the early stages of building it, the network has the least value. These early stages of business transformation are also the most susceptible to misunderstanding by those who have never used the technology and do not yet understand its capabilities. The grand vision of a connected company—the feeling of being part of "one firm" and seamless communication—is extremely valuable. But it is soft value.

In environments where cultural transformation has not yet reached a crisis point, you will not be able to make a business case that can stick. Instead, change management is easier in clear, controllable groups. Once you get through the first stages of the implementation, expanding throughout the company is substantially easier.

Though all of the innovation in social technologies is not done, the demands of the Red Queen's race won't go away. The pressure to work harder, process information faster, and stay ahead of—if not maintain pace with—competitors continues unless you use social business technology to break the cycle. Don't miss your opportunity to stop running in place and start racing toward the future.

NOTES

CHAPTER 1

1. "Oldest Tool Use and Meat Eating Revealed," *Museum of Natural History*, August 12, 2010, http://www.nhm.ac.uk/about-us/news/2010/august/oldest-tool-use-and-meat-eating-revealed75831.html (September 14, 2012).
2. Ray Kurzweil, *The Singularity Is Near: When Humans Transcend Biology* (New York: Penguin, 2006).
3. Pony Express History, Official Pony Express, http://www.officialponyexpress.org/index_files/Page860.htm (June 13, 2012).
4. Ray Kurzweil, op. cit.
5. Ibid.
6. PriceWaterhouseCoopers LLP, "Transforming into a Social Enterprise," August 2011.
7. Lewis Carroll, *Through the Looking-Glass, and What Alice Found There* (London: MacMillan, 1871).
8. Authors' interview with Allison Kaplan on December 23, 2012.
9. "Sheryl Sandberg: By the Book," *New York Times*, March 14, 2013, http://www.nytimes.com/2013/03/17/books/review/sheryl-sandberg-by-the-book.html?ref=books.
10. Quotations from authors' interview with Jesper Sørensen on August 7, 2012.
11. Seth Godin, presentation at Gartner Customer 360 Summit, March 2012.
12. Quotations from authors' interview with Jesper Sørensen on August 7, 2012.
13. Content from authors' interview with Andy Sernovitz on September 25, 2012.
14. Amir Efrati, "Kleiner Perkins' View of the Future of Tech," December 19, 2012, *Wall Street Journal*, http://online.wsj.com/article/SB10001424127887324407504578185381152508470.html?mod=WSJ_hps_MIDDLE_Video_Third (December 20, 2012).

15. Marc Andreessen, "Why Software Is Eating the World," *Wall Street Journal*, August 20, 2011, http://online.wsj.com/article/SB10001424053111 90348090457651225091562946O.html (September 10, 2012).

16. Dion Hinchcliffe, "The 'Big Five' IT Trends of the Next Half Decade: Mobile, Social, Cloud, Consumerization, and Big Data," *ZDNet*, October 2, 2011, http://www.zdnet.com/blog/hinchcliffe/the-big-five-it-trends-of-the-next-half-decade-mobile-social-cloud-consumerization-and-big-data/1811 (April 25, 2012).

17. Aaron Ricadela, "In Buying Mint, Intuit Looks to Revitalize," *Businessweek*, September 14, 2009, http://www.businessweek.com/technology/content/sep2009/tc20090914_208171.htm (April 26, 2012).

18. Aarti Shahani, "Electronic Arts Faces New Gaming Challenges," KQED: *The California Report*, April 26, 2012, http://www.californiareport.org/archive/R201204260850/b (April 30, 2012).

19. Dominic Orr, "Competing with Giants: It's All About Speed," Stanford Entrepreneurial Thought Leader Series, October 17, 2007, http://ecorner.stanford.edu/authorMaterialInfo.html?mid=1864 (August 24, 2012).

20. Sohrab Vossoughi, "Strategy, Context, and the Decline of Sony," *Harvard Business Review–HBR Blog Network*, April 25, 2012, http://blogs.hbr.org/cs/2012/04/strategy_context_and_the_decli.html?awid =7768449636617700932–3271 (April 30, 2012).

21. Kasra Ferdows, Michael A. Lewis, and Jose A.D. Machuca, "Zara's Secret for Fast Fashion," *Harvard Business School Working Knowledge*, February 21, 2005, http://hbswk.hbs.edu/archive/4652.html (June 14, 2012).

22. Suzy Hansen, "How Zara Grew into the World's Largest Fashion Retailer," *New York Times*, November 9, 2012, http://www.nytimes.com/2012/11/11/magazine/how-zara-grew-into-the-worlds-largest-fashion-retailer.html?pagewanted=2&ref=style (November 9, 2012).

23. Kasra Ferdows, Michael A. Lewis, and Jose A.D. Machuca, op. cit.

24. Adrianne Pasquarelli, "Fashion Gets Fast," *Crain's New York Business*, May 13, 2012, http://www.crainsnewyork.com/article/20120513/RETAIL_APPAREL/305139979, (June 14, 2012).

25. Greg Petro, "The Future of Fashion Retailing: The Zara Approach (Part 2 of 3)," October 25, 2012, *Forbes*, http://www.forbes.com/sites/gregpetro/2012/10/25/the-future-of-fashion-retailing-the-zara-approach-part-2-of-3/ (December 18, 2012).

26. Dean Faust, "Frederick W. Smith: No Overnight Success," *Businessweek*, September 20, 2004, http://www.businessweek.com/magazine/content/04_38/b3900032_mz072.htm (June 13, 2012).

27. The Standard & Poors 500 (S&P 500) includes companies that are selected by an S team of analysts and economists at Standard & Poors. The S&P 500 is a market value weighted index; each stock's weight is proportionate to its market value.

28. Richard Foster and Sarah Kaplan, *Creative Destruction: Why Companies That Are Built to Last Underperform the Market—And How to Successfully Transform Them* (New York: Doubleday, 2001).

29. Ibid.

30. Ibid.

31. Claudia Deutsch, "At Kodak, Some Old Things Are New Again," *New York Times*, May 2, 2008, http://www.nytimes.com/2008/05/02/technology/02kodak.html (April 17, 2012).

32. Chunka Mui, "How Kodak Failed," *Forbes*, January 18, 2012, http://www.forbes.com/sites/chunkamui/2012/01/18/how-kodak-failed/ (April 17, 2012).

33. Claudia Deutsch, "Chief Says Kodak Is Pointed in the Right Direction," *New York Times*, December 25, 1999, http://www.nytimes.com/1999/12/25/business/chief-says-kodak-is-pointed-in-the-right-direction.html?src=pm (April 17, 2012).

34. Mike Orcutt, "The Pressure's on for Intel," *MIT Technology Review*, November 9, 2012, http://www.technologyreview.com/news/507011/the-pressures-on-for-intel/ (November 26, 2012).

35. Don Clark and Joann S. Lublin, "Intel CEO Will Retire Early," *Wall Street Journal*, November 19, 2012, http://online.wsj.com/article/SB10001424127887323353204578128832438077830.html?KEYWORDS=intel (November 26, 2012).

36. Ibid.

37. Jay Yarow, "Here's What Steve Ballmer Thought About the iPhone Five Years Ago," *Business Insider*, June 29, 2012, http://www.businessinsider.com/heres-what-steve-ballmer-thought-about-the-iphone-five-years-ago-2012-6 (July 2, 2012).

38. Ibid.

39. John Paczkowski, "The iPhone Doesn't Appeal to Business Customers at All?" *All Things D*, December 2, 2008, http://allthingsd.com/20081202/no-the-iphone-doesnt-appeal-to-business-customers-at-all/ (July 2, 2012).

40. Richard Foster and Sarah Kaplan, *Creative Destruction: Why Companies That Are Built to Last Underperform the Market—and How to Successfully Transform Them* (New York: Doubleday, 2001).

41. Paul Sen, "Steve Jobs: The Lost Interview," 2011, John Gau Productions Ltd.

42. James Allworth, "Steve Jobs Solved the Innovator's Dilemma," October 24, 2011, *HBR Blog Network*, http://blogs.hbr.org/cs/2011/10/steve_jobs_solved_the_innovato.html (August 15, 2012).

43. Aaron Levie in conversation with Tony Zingale, JiveWorld 2012, October 11, 2012.

44. Aaron Levie, "Rise of the Enterprise 'Toys,'" *TechCrunch.com*, July 1, 2012, http://techcrunch.com/2012/07/01/rise-of-the-enterprise-toys/ (July 2, 2012).

45. Michael Totten, "The History of the Seattle Underground," www.helium.com, April 4, 2011, http://www.helium.com/items/1241664-the-history-of-the-seattle-underground (June 28, 2012).

46. Amy Liu, "Rebirth on the Bayou? Lessons from New Orleans and the Gulf Coast," Brookings Institution, August 29, 2011, http://www.brookings.edu/opinions/2011/0826_resilience_hurricane_liu.aspx (April 30, 2012).

47. Vito Racanelli, "The Culture Changer," *Barron's*, March 10, 2012, http://online.barrons.com/article/SB50001424052748704759704577265510752521758.html#articleTabs_article%3D2 (June 27, 2012).

48. Ibid.

49. Quotation from authors' interview with Nilofer Merchant on July 30, 2013.

CHAPTER 2

1. Quotations from authors' interview with Ian MacLeod on August 21, 2012.

2. Gartner.com, http://www.gartner.com/it-glossary/social-technologies/.

3. Mary Meeker and Liang Wu, "2012 Internet Trends (Update)," December 3, 2012, http://www.kpcb.com/insights/2012-internet-trends-update (December 19, 2012).

4. Aaron Levie in conversation with Tony Zingale, JiveWorld 2012, October 11, 2012.

5. Mary Meeker and Liang Wu, "2012 Internet Trends (Update)," December 3, 2012, http://www.kpcb.com/insights/2012-internet-trends-update (December 19, 2012).

6. "Digital Data Explosion to Drive Growth in the World Network Attached Storage Devices Market," Global Industry Analysts, April 5, 2012, http://www.prweb.com/releases/network_attached_storage/NAS_devices/prweb9373388.htm, (September 20, 2012).

7. Joseph Walker, "Meet the New Boss: Big Data," *Wall Street Journal*, September 20, 2012, http://online.wsj.com/article/SB10000872396390443890304578006252019616768.html?mod=WSJ_hps_MIDDLENexttoWhatsNewsFifth (September 20, 2012).

8. David Gutelius, "Join Me: Big Data Meets Social Analytics," JiveTalks, June 21, 2011, https://community.jivesoftware.com/community/jivetalks/blog/2011/06/21/join-me-big-data-meets-social-analytics-at-enterprise-20 (October 15, 2012).

9. Quotations from authors' interviews with David Gutelius in 2012.

10. Authors' interview with Joe Kraus on August 20, 2012.

11. Ibid.

12. Quotation from authors' interview with Anna-Christina Douglas on June 26, 2013.

13. Quotations from authors' interviews with David Gutelius in 2012.

14. Jordan Cohen, "What Manufacturing Taught Me About Business," HBR Blog Network, February 4, 2013, http://blogs.hbr.org/cs/2013/02/what_manufacturing_taught_me_a.html?utm_campaign=Socialflow&utm_source=Socialflow&utm_medium=Tweet/.

CHAPTER 3

1. Quotation from authors' interview with Marc Andreessen on September 11, 2012.

2. Quotations from authors' interview with Gerry Myers and Jon Bidwell on October 10, 2012.

3. Quotations from authors' interview with Andy Wang on June 22, 2012.

4. William Barnett and Sara Gaviser Leslie, "User-Generated Content Systems at Intuit (B)," Stanford Graduate School of Business, May 3, 2010, https://gsbapps.stanford.edu/cases/documents/E381B.pdf.

5. Quotation from authors' interview with Scott Brown on October 10, 2012.

6. Steven VanRoekel, "The Mobile Opportunity," White House Office of Management and Budget, January 12, 2012, http://www.whitehouse.gov/blog/2012/01/12/mobile-opportunity.

7. "How Can You Build a Growth Factory?" Innosight, www.innosight.com/impact-stories/procter-and-gamble-growth-factory-case-study.cfm.

8. Proctor & Gamble Connect + Develop, http://www.pg.com/connect_develop/index.shtml (November 30, 2012).

9. Pete Cashmore, "From the Arab Spring to Sopa: The Future of Power Is Us," Mashable, February 1, 2012, http://mashable.com/2012/02/01/arab-spring-sopa-davos/.

10. Mathew Ingram, "Was What Happened in Tunisia a Twitter Revolution?" Gigaom, January 14, 2011, http://gigaom.com/2011/01/14/was-what-happened-in-tunisia-a-twitter-revolution/.

11. Malcolm Gladwell and Clay Shirky, "Do Social Media Make Protests Possible?" Foreign Affairs, May-June 2011, http://www.foreignaffairs.com/articles/67325/malcolm-gladwell-and-clay-shirky/from-innovation-to-revolution.

12. Quotations from authors' interviews with David Gutelius in 2012.

13. McKinsey Global Institute analysis and Scott Beardsley, Bradford C. Johnson, and James Manyika, "Competitive Advantage from Better Interactions," *McKinsey Quarterly*, May 2006; Bradford C. Johnson, James M. Manyika, and Lareina A. Yee, "The Next Revolution in Interactions," *McKinsey Quarterly*, November 2005; and Patrick Butler, Ted W. Hall, Alistair M. Hanna, Lenny Mendonca, Byron Auguste, James Manyika, and Anupam Sahay, "A Revolution in Interaction," *McKinsey Quarterly*, February 1997.

14. Robert Coram, "The Fighter Pilot Who Changed the Art of Air Warfare," www.aviation-history.com, http://www.aviation-history.com/airmen/boyd.htm.

15. Alexander Budzier and Bent Flyvbjerg, "Why Your IT Project May Be Riskier Than You Think," *Harvard Business Review*, September 2011.

CHAPTER 4

1. The value creation statistics cited in this chapter are results of the Jive customer survey conducted by a top-tier management consultancy in November 2012.

2. Quotation from authors' interview with Marc Andreessen, September 11, 2012.

3. Jeffrey Cohn, Jon Katzenbach, and Gus Vlak, "Finding and Grooming Breakthrough Innovators," *Harvard Business Review*, December 2008.

4. Ray Wang, "How to Engage Your Customers," May 9, 2012, HBR Blog Network, http://blogs.hbr.org/cs/2012/05/how_to_engage_your_customers_a.html.

5. "2012 Global Workforce Study: At a Glance," Towers Watson, 2012, http://www.towerswatson.com/assets/pdf/7564/TowersWatson-GWS-At-a-Glance-NA-2012-25644.pdf (August 3, 2012).

6. Nikki Blacksmith and Jim Harter, "Majority of American Workers Not Engaged in Their Jobs," Gallup, October 28, 2011, http://www.gallup.com/poll/150383/Majority-American-Workers-Not-Engaged-Jobs.aspx (July 9, 2012).

7. Thomas H. Davenport, Jeanne Harris, and Jeremy Shapiro, "Competing on Talent Acquisition," October 2010, *Harvard Business Review*, http://hbr.org/2010/10/competing-on-talent-analytics/ar/1 (August 3, 2012).

8. James K. Harter, Frank L. Schmidt, Emily A. Killham, and Sangeeta Agrawal, "Q12® Meta-Analysis: The Relationship Between Engagement at Work and Organizational Outcomes," August 2009, Gallup Inc., http://www.gallup.com/consulting/126806/q12-meta-analysis.aspx (July 9, 2012).

9. Nikki Blacksmith and Jim Harter, "Majority of American Workers Not Engaged in Their Jobs," op. cit.

10. Report completed for Jive Software by independent top three management consulting firm.

11. *McKinsey Quarterly* survey in 2006 of 800 senior executives from across industries and geographies in organizations with revenues of at least $500 million; "Wells Fargo Chairman Eyes Possible Acquisitions," Reuters, September 18, 2008.

12. The cases in this chapter are from the Jive customer survey conducted in November 2012 or interviews with Jive customers.

13. The company had already implemented a social business platform for another purpose: strategic alignment/collaboration.

14. Quotations from authors' interviews with Scott Tweedy and Will Rose on October 11, 2012.

15. Ibid.

16. McKinsey & Company's Complexity KIP, 2012.

17. Report completed for Jive Software by independent top-three management consulting firm.

18. McKinsey Global Institute, "The Social Economy: Unlocking Value and Productivity Through Social Technologies," McKinsey & Company, July 2012.

CHAPTER 5

1. If you are implementing a social platform for a workgroup/pain implementation, you don't need a lot of context. You just need to know that the product is working.
2. *New State Ice Co. v. Liebmann*, 285 U.S. 262 (1932), http://caselaw. lp.findlaw.com/scripts/getcase.pl?court=us&vol=285&invol=262.
3. Charles Duhigg, *The Power of Habit: Why We Do What We Do in Life and Business* (New York: Random House, 2012), pp. 17–19, 145–146.
4. LDAP refers to the Lightweight Directory Access Protocol, an Internet protocol that e-mail and other programs use to look up information from a server.
5. Daniel Pink, *Drive: The Surprising Truth About What Motivates Us* (New York: Riverhead Books, 2011).
6. Quotations from authors' interview with Rajat Paharia on July 5, 2012.
7. Quotations from authors' interview with John Stepper on November 15, 2012.

CHAPTER 6

1. Deloitte, "Social Software for Business Performance," 2012, p. 4, http://www.deloitte.com/view/en_US/us/Industries/technology/ e9c1b39fb701e210VgnVCM3000001c56f00aRCRD.htm#.
2. "Predicts 2013: Social and Collaboration Go Deeper and Wider," Gartner, November 28, 2012, http://www.gartner.com/id=2254316 (January 7, 2013).
3. Jacques Bughin and Michael Chi, "Evolution of the Networked Enterprise," McKinsey & Company, 2013.
4. Quotations from authors' interview with Steve Kahl on August 21, 2012.
5. Quotation from authors' interview with Greg D'Alesandre on July 19, 2012.
6. Quotations from authors' interview with Ian McCleod on August 21, 2012.
7. Quotation from authors' interview with Greg D'Alesandre on July 19, 2012.
8. Ibid.
9. Quotation from authors' interview with Scott Johnston on July 23, 2012.
10. Ibid.

11. Quotation from authors' interview with Andy Sernovitz on September 24, 2012.

12. McKinsey Global Institute, "The Social Economy: Unlocking Value and Productivity Through Social Technologies," McKinsey & Company, July 2012.

CHAPTER 7

1. "History of AT&T," www.corp.att.com, http://www.corp.att.com/history/history1.html.

2. Quotations from authors' interview with Matt Tucker on January 25, 2013.

3. FINRA, Regulatory Notice 10–06, http://www.finra.org/web/groups/industry/@ip/@reg/@notice/documents/notices/p120779.pdf.

4. Carolyn Fraser, "Worth the Investment—Social Media for the Financial Services Industry," January 28, 2011, http://www.7summitsagency.com/uncategorized/worth-the-investment-social-media-for-the-financial-services-industry/.

5. Quotations from authors' interview with John Stepper on November 16, 2012.

6. Quotations from authors' interview with Scott Ross on November 16, 2012.

7. Quotations from authors' interview with Jesper Sørensen on August 7, 2012.

8. Quotations from authors' interview with Scott Johnston on July 23, 2012.

9. Michael Arrington, "Wave Goodbye to Google Wave," TechCrunch.com, August 10, 2010, http://techcrunch.com/2010/08/04/wave-goodbye-to-google-wave/.

10. Christina Warren, "Lessons Google Can Learn from Wave's Failure," Mashable, August 6, 2010, http://mashable.com/2010/08/06/google-wave-lessons/ (July 17, 2012).

11. Eric Eldon, "After a Breakout 2011, Yammer Works on a Big New Funding Round," Techcrunch.com, January 5, 2012.

12. Authors' interview with security executive on June 28, 2012.

13. Bud Methaisel, "The CIO's Role in Social Enterprise Strategy," PwC Technology Forecast, http://www.pwc.com/us/en/technology-forecast/2011/issue3/features/feature-cio-role-social-enterprise-strategy.jhtml.

INDEX